FROM FOOT SAFARIS TO HELICOPTERS

FROM FOOT SAFARIS TO HELICOPTERS

100 years of the Davis family in missions

ART DAVIS

iUniverse, Inc.
Bloomington

From Foot Safaris to Helicopters
100 years of the Davis family in missions

Copyright © 2011 by Art Davis.

Cover photos:
The top photo shows Dr. Elwood Davis with his two-year-old son Linnell and porters and a mule on safari in Kenya in 1915.
In the bottom photo Art Davis sits under the tree to share the message of Jesus on a helicopter safari in northern Kenya in the 1990s.

All rights reserved. No part of this book may be used or reproduced by any means, graphic, electronic, or mechanical, including photocopying, recording, taping or by any information storage retrieval system without the written permission of the publisher except in the case of brief quotations embodied in critical articles and reviews.

iUniverse books may be ordered through booksellers or by contacting:

iUniverse
1663 Liberty Drive
Bloomington, IN 47403
www.iuniverse.com
1-800-Authors (1-800-288-4677)

Because of the dynamic nature of the Internet, any web addresses or links contained in this book may have changed since publication and may no longer be valid. The views expressed in this work are solely those of the author and do not necessarily reflect the views of the publisher, and the publisher hereby disclaims any responsibility for them.

Any people depicted in stock imagery provided by Thinkstock are models, and such images are being used for illustrative purposes only.
Certain stock imagery © Thinkstock.

ISBN: 978-1-4620-6760-2 (sc)
ISBN: 978-1-4620-6761-9 (ebk)

Printed in the United States of America

iUniverse rev. date: 12/17/2011

Contents

Dedication vii
Author's Note ix
Foreword xi
Preface xv
Chapter 1: How it All Began 1
Chapter 2: Early Kenya Days 8
Chapter 3: Life in the Roaring Twenties and Thirties 31
Chapter 4: Challenges of the Forties, Fifties and Sixties 63
Chapter 5: The Third Generation Takes Over 90
Chapter 6: Hunting Adventures 152
Chapter 7: Key Partners 173
Conclusion 181
Bibliography 185
Glossary of African Words 187
The Davis Family Tree 189

DEDICATION

This book is dedicated to the life, ministry and honor of our beloved grandparents, Dr. Elwood and Bernice Davis.

AUTHOR'S NOTE

This book shows how the Gospel first came to Kenya with the early missionaries, under adverse circumstances and with financial struggles. The first section of the book focuses on the pioneering work of my grandparents, Dr. Elwood and Bernice Davis, and my parents, Linnell and Martha Davis. The second section shows how the Gospel continued to spread through the next generation, with an emphasis on reaching the Pokot people.

Among the first parties of various mission groups, some missionaries died of malaria—Peter Cameron Scott of Africa Inland Mission (AIM) along with two others of the first party of eight—while others were killed in physical attacks like the Houghtons, Methodist missionaries killed by Maasai warriors at Golbanti, their mission station on the Tana River.

When my grandfather, Dr. Elwood Davis, entered Kenya in 1911, the fledgling Africa Inland Mission had a few stations in East Africa, but were already exploring into Congo, Central African Republic and Sudan. Very few missionaries died in this generation.

Dr. Elwood served as a medical doctor and administrator and finance officer. In common with other early missionary pioneers, he didn't receive a large salary, travel allowance and good retirement benefits. He and his fellow workers were mostly God-driven paupers.

A generation later, my parents had more income, better roads, infrastructure, available medical services and a more highly developed mission board.

Our third generation came along in the late 1960s and 1970s with even better financial support and with more interested donors helping with community and church development projects.

By the 1980s missionaries lived in nice houses, drove newer and sturdier vehicles, returned to their home countries more often and went on holidays to game parks and to Kenya's coast. But this more comfortable lifestyle did not make them any less hard working or committed.

In this book I attempt to show the spiritual impact missionaries have had on the national peoples and their own personal spiritual experiences as they served others.

Art Davis,
Naivasha, Kenya
2011

FOREWORD

I first met Art Davis at an Evangelical Literature Overseas (ELO) conference in February 1963 at Winona Lake, Indiana. Art, a missionary kid from Kenya, hoped to be a third generation missionary in that East African land. I had also grown up on the mission field in the Philippines, the son of the world literacy pioneer, Frank C. Laubach. From our very first meeting at Winona Lake, we 'mish kids' had a lot in common.

I had started a literacy training program in Syracuse, New York. Art came to my graduate program at Syracuse University's School of Journalism because I told him literacy and journalism training would be a strong help in his missions work. During his studies in Syracuse, Art and another young man, John Stauffer, and I forged a friendship that has lasted 48 years.

Literacy training involves studying methods of teaching literacy. A very important part of any literacy program is the provision of ultra-easy reading materials for new readers. We call men and women 'new readers' when they are learning to read in their own language.

I had traveled with my father Frank Laubach to a number of African nations in the late 1940s. I had seen how a nation might improve its literacy rate with a mass literacy campaign. But if there were no easy reading materials for the 'new readers' many new readers lapsed back into illiteracy.

Art, training for the mission field, was interested in learning to write the saving Christian message along with practical subjects, like keeping malaria-carrying mosquitoes off babies, or drilling wells for safe drinking water. In my training I emphasized: "Keep choosing simple words. Keep sentences short. Keep your writing easy! Easy! Easy!"

Our friend John Stauffer earned a PhD in Communications at Syracuse University. He taught at a US business college, and at various times taught at universities in Kenya and South Africa. He has visited Art and Mary Ellen Davis in Africa on numerous occasions to help with their mission work.

All three of us—Art, John and I visited Kenya in 1968. The organization my father had started, Laubach Literacy International, was organizing *AfroLit,* an organization to serve literacy programs in many countries. A group of literacy missionaries from a dozen African countries gathered in Nairobi for a week-long conference. *AfroLit* served Africa well for 20 years.

Art Davis married Mary Ellen Huber of Lancaster, Pennsylvania in 1965 and they began their mission life in 1972. Over the years I have traveled to Africa numerous times, and have met with Art and Mary Ellen in Kenya on several occasions.

For about 30 years the Davises have worked among the East Pokot people in the north of Kenya. More than 30 churches have been planted with eight pastors and 12 evangelists.

I have kept in touch with the Davises by letters and photographs over the years, and have admired their pioneering missionary work. Art Davis has penned a stirring narrative, telling about the four generations of Davis family members who have served, not only in Africa, but also in South America.

Art and Mary Ellen have a son, Jeff, and a daughter, Karen, working as missionaries with their families in Kenya and Tanzania respectively. Kristin, another daughter, currently based in Switzerland, is executive secretary of a global forum of rural advisory services for farmers. They represent the fourth generation of the admirable Davis missionary family.

It is my pleasure to recommend this book to all who are interested in a thrilling story that stretches over one hundred years.

From Foot Safaris to Helicopters

Dr. Bob Laubach
Syracuse, New York
November 2010

Dr. Bob Laubach, son of world-renowned literacy teacher Frank Laubach, in front of his parents' gravestone.

PREFACE

"Come on, Papa. Come on! I see Jesus coming down the path to meet us."

Little David, six years old, was walking with his father, Van V. Eddings, near their home in Carúpano, Venezuela. David, who had not been healthy since birth, had some unusual malfunction that wouldn't allow his digestive system to work properly.

Van and his wife Gara had treated David carefully and tenderly for those six years and he enjoyed his short life, playing and doing things like other kids.

But on the day he saw a vision of Jesus coming to meet him, David came to the end of his earthly life and went to live with Jesus forever. A few days later he was buried in the church cemetery far from his parents' homeland, but forever at home with Jesus in his heavenly home.

This heart-rending experience would have sent many people packing for home and decrying the fact that if they had remained in America they could have enjoyed the best medical care available, and lived near a cousin, Dr. Lucina Turner, who was a physician. But Van and Gara accepted the loss of their son David and redoubled their efforts preaching about Jesus to the people of Venezuela. In spite of this tragic loss, they continued in Venezuela for another 40 years, believing that showing others the way to eternal life in Jesus was their life calling.

There is only one explanation for that! "Christ in them, their hope of glory." (Colossians 1:27).

Van and Gara Eddings with Martha (later Linnell Davis's wife) and her brother David who died in Venezuela at age 6.

The Eddings' daughter, Martha, my mother, served in Kenya as a missionary for nearly 40 years. The Eddings also had a set of twins, later born in the US, Frederic and Cedric. Frederic died of an infection when just days old; Cedric together with his wife Florene served in Venezuela as missionaries.

Van and Gara Eddings were my grandparents, and David, if he had lived, would have been my uncle. My grandparents weren't the only missionaries to lose a child while working overseas. I greatly admired the prayer life of Dr. Frank C. Laubach, known as the apostle to the illiterates. He gave me a signed copy of his moving book **Living Words**. In the front he wrote, "Prayer lets God set you ablaze." Dr. Laubach was a great man of prayer, who himself was a man set ablaze by his prayer life. Dr. Frank's son, Dr. Bob Laubach, shared a moving personal story with me that helped me understand more about his father's prayer life. Bob was the last born of four boys, but he didn't learn until he was in college that he had three older brothers who had all died either at childbirth or in infancy.

What a blow that must have been to a godly family who from 1916 to the early 1940s had given their lives for God in the mission field of the Philippines.

Only God knows how many thousands of people came to believe in Jesus Christ because they were taught to read by the Laubachs and their students spread all over the world.

While Dr. Laubach taught literacy in the Philippines and led people to faith in Christ, my grandparents on my mother's side were taking the Gospel of Jesus Christ to Venezuela and my grandparents on my father's side went to Africa to tell the people there about God's love.

This book tells the story of our family's four generations of missionaries—both in Africa and in South America. As our family has worked to share Jesus to those who did not know him, we have suffered setbacks and endured sacrifices. But we have been privileged to see God work in building his church around the world.

Chapter 1

How it All Began

Nellie Arilla Van Vleck, affectionately known as Our Little Grandma, was the only child of Civil War hero Colonel Carter Van Vleck. As part of the 78th Illinois Infantry he rode next to General John Sherman in the battle for Atlanta. A sniper tried to kill the general, but instead the bullet hit 34-year-old Colonel Van Vleck in the head and knocked him off his horse. He lived for four more days and his wife Arilla traveled from Macomb, Illinois, arriving in Atlanta to spend time with him and hear his last words.

Their only daughter, 12 year-old Nellie, had been a sickly child and was not expected to reach adulthood. Nellie did live, growing up in a God-fearing home.

Nellie Van Vleck married George Eddings and they raised their children and grandchildren in the ways of God through Bible teaching and church activities. Lucina, the oldest, became the first female osteopathic physician and was known for her kindness to patients who were unable to pay, treating them day and night. She married Arthur Turner; they were the parents of Sylvia and an adopted son, Hal.

Carter, the second born, went west to look for gold. He also knew some Hollywood people well and spent time with them. Unfortunately, he was shot and killed by another gold-digger who took over his claims.

Ruth, another daughter, married Clifford Cunningham and they had two sons, Van and Clifford.

Van, the youngest (and my maternal grandfather), later became a missionary in Venezuela.

George and Nellie (Little Grandma) Eddings, the author's great grandmother.

"Little Grandma was a godly woman and did a lot of praying," her granddaughter Sylvia remembers. No doubt the prayers of Little Grandma were answered on behalf of Sylvia as well. Sylvia had married George Woodgates, the firstborn son of English immigrants. As they were driving home from a little Baptist church in southern California in 1942, George kept repeating this phrase: "If it IS really true, who WOULDN'T want to believe it?" He was referring, of course, to the free gift of eternal life offered by God through the death of His Son, Jesus Christ, on Calvary's cross.

That evening when they returned to church, George had a chance to share his newfound faith in Christ. He later went on to study at the Episcopal Seminary at the University of California; he pastored churches in California, Illinois and Massachusetts before being made the Director of Christian Education for the Episcopal Church of the USA.

Another of Little Grandma's prayers was answered when her son Van studied at the Bible Institute of Los Angeles (BIOLA) and was an active member of the Fisherman's Club, a group who sponsored evangelistic work by the students into the outlying communities.

After graduation, Van and his new wife Gara Shaw, daughter of a brothel owner in Kansas, moved to New Mexico to pastor a small congregation. In 1911, during their first year, they received a letter with a plea for help from a former classmate who had gone to Venezuela. Mrs. Elinor Bjornstad wrote this tribute concerning the Eddings when Gara passed away in 1992 at the age of 100. "When the mailman left that lone letter at the dilapidated parsonage in New Mexico, he never imagined the impact it would have on countless lives. It was postmarked Caracas, Venezuela.

"Opening the letter, the young pastor and his wife were instantly challenged. 'My right-hand man has died of fever. Come and help. Step out on faith.'"

Van and Gara responded immediately to this plea and within months set sail for Venezuela. Together with their co-worker, they got the work going. But soon they realized they needed more support and more workers. They returned to the US and in less than a year went back to Venezuela with more support and another couple.

Shortly afterwards, they founded the Orinoco River Mission with some well-known men such as Bible teacher J. Vernon McGee and Christian businessmen on their board.

The Eddings served a lifetime of ministry in their beloved Venezuela. Their son Cedric married Florene McKenrick, whose father Fred McKenrick went as a missionary to Kenya in 1905. Cedric and Florene went as missionaries to Venezuela in 1950. Van and Gara's daughter Martha married Linnell Davis; they went to Kenya as missionaries in 1938. Three of their four sons—Van, Art, and Ray also returned to Kenya as missionaries and now two of Art's children are in Africa as well as Ray's son.

As the Eddings' children were being raised in California, the Davis family was living in the New Jersey and Pennsylvania areas of the United States.

Titus Davis was pastor of the Presbyterian Church in Bound Brook, New Jersey, and also served churches in Pennsylvania and Washington, DC. He and his wife Arvilla reared six children in the parsonages where they lived.

Titus and Arvilla's son Elwood Linnell graduated *Phi Beta Kappa* from Rutgers College in 1902 before going on to study medicine at the Medical School of the University of Pennsylvania in Philadelphia. He also studied homeopathic medicine at the Hahnemann College of Medicine in the same city.

In March 1906, Elwood attended a Student Volunteer Convention in Nashville, Tennessee. While there, he committed his life to Christ fully and by signing the Student Declaration Card promised God he would go to a foreign mission field.

But making this decision was not an easy thing to do. Elwood notes in his diary March 3, 1906, Saturday, "I had a talk with Wm J Miller, Jr, regarding my becoming a Student Volunteer. As far as I am concerned I am perfectly willing, but there is one who always causes me to hesitate. I promised to think and pray over it and to try to bring Gertrude to see that there is a need for me in the mission field."

On March 4, 1906 he continues: "As I left the meeting . . . how much happier and easier in mind I do feel now that I am a Volunteer. As I am to prepare myself for foreign missionary work,

I have something definite to live and work for. Thank God for His unspeakable goodness to this servant."

When Elwood returned to his studies in Philadelphia and shared with his fiancée Gertrude (their wedding was to take place in June) that they were going to Africa, her response was, "Then you are going by yourself!"

He was sorely disappointed, as he had really come to love Gertrude, his 'brown-eyed beauty,' as he fondly referred to her. But so strong was his commitment that he forged ahead with his plans to go as a missionary doctor to Africa without her. He then began a deeper relationship with Bernice Conger, a nurse from the Hahnemann College of Medicine in Philadelphia from which he had recently graduated. On November 12, 1910, two weeks before sailing for Africa under the Africa Inland Mission (AIM), they were married. Bernice Conger, RN, was to be his lifetime partner for nearly 40 years in service to Africa. She too had felt God's call to a lifetime of missionary service.

Fred McKenrick was a missionary in Kenya in 1909 when former US president Teddy Roosevelt (left) visited AIM's director Charles Hurlburt (right) at Kijabe.

Teddy Roosevelt in camp in the Kedong Valley below Kijabe in 1909.

Former US President Teddy Roosevelt laying the Kiambogo cornerstone at Kijabe in 1909. Roosevelt's head is visible above the lady's hat and AIM's director Charles Hurlburt is next on the right.

Early AIM missionaries on an oxcart safari.

CHAPTER 2

Early Kenya Days

After spending six weeks onboard ship, Elwood and Bernice arrived in Mombasa, Kenya, on January 11, 1911, to begin their almost 40 years of missionary service. That same evening they traveled by train to Nairobi.

On their arrival in Nairobi they completed the necessary paperwork and were assigned to Machakos, the main mission station of AIM at that time.

Elwood and Bernice's house at Machakos about 1912.

Two years later, on February 12, 1913, while they were still living in Machakos and doing itinerant evangelism and medical work from there, Linnell, their first son was born. That same year they moved to Mukaa to take over for missionaries going on furlough.

Elwood and Bernice with baby Linnell at Machakos in 1913.

While at Mukaa, they improved their grasp of the Kamba language and young Linnell picked up the language even more rapidly. Dr. Johnstone, a fellow missionary, remembers hearing Linnell singing himself to sleep with a hymn from the Kamba hymnbook called, *"Break thou the bread of life, dear Lord to me . . . ."* And Linnell was only two years old!

Elwood and Bernice (back left), C.F. Johnston (middle), Mrs. Johnston (bottom left) possibly Mr. and Mrs. Waechter (right).

Elwood Davis and two-year-old Linnell at Mukaa in about 1915.

From Foot Safaris to Helicopters

The first Machakos church under the mumbu tree in about 1915.

In 1916 the Davises left Mukaa and returned to the US for a one-year furlough. They traveled by sea from Mombasa aboard the *SS Pundua*. Since the number of passengers was few, they were moved into a first class cabin in Class C, enjoying their three berth cabin that was more nicely equipped than the third class cabin in which they started. They had a bit of a scare as three year old Linnell fell down seven steps, suffering a severe contusion on the left side of his head. He vomited considerably but was better by that same evening.

This intended one year furlough turned into nearly four years due to the First World War. Dr. Davis spent much of his time serving at three different military hospitals in Virginia and Tennessee. While in the US, a second son, Philip, was born, on October 11, 1916, in Scranton, Pennsylvania.

They headed back to Kenya on February 20, 1920, aboard the *SS Madison*. Elwood had a penchant for details and noted the *Madison* was a 10,000 ton vessel, 430 feet long and 54 feet 2 inches wide.

Reaching Mombasa on May 1, they took the train upcountry that evening. By next morning they had reached Makindu where they had breakfast and later ate lunch at Kiu. It was a delight for them to see many game animals along the way. They spent that night in the New Stanley Hotel, Nairobi. Elwood commented that Nairobi looked 'natural' to them and it was good to be in British East Africa again.

A church meeting under a mumbu tree in Ukambani in the 1920s.

They were booked on the 4.10 pm train to Kijabe, but that was delayed until 8 pm because of an accident on the rail line. When they arrived at Kijabe Station it was midnight; Mr. Propst and some porters met them with a two-wheeled cart pulled by two mules. Bernice and the boys rode in the cart with Miss Jaeger (another missionary); Mr. Propst and Elwood rode the mules and it was 2 am when they reached Kijabe mission station—a distance of only three miles!

They dove into their mission work and enjoyed 'five glorious years of work with both sons, Linnell and Philip, at home.'

Elwood and Bernice were assigned to Kijabe, as they were asked to lead the medical work there. Over the next number of years, they raised funds for what was then called Theodora Hospital and worked long hours in the understaffed hospital. Most of Elwood's Africa career was spent running this hospital, later named Kijabe

Medical Center Mission and now called AIC Kijabe Hospital. Dr. Davis also built a reputation as a skilled surgeon.

Dr. Elwood Davis with a Kikuyu couple looking for their lost son in the forest near Kijabe in the 1920s.

Medical missionaries, Elwood and Bernice certainly had a double barrel of fulfillment while ministering to the bodies and souls of the Kenyans and Europeans living in the area. "Miss Gladys Clarke had been so really sick for many months and was so discouraged she wanted to go home. But thanks to medicine and care for four months at Kijabe she fully recovered and was able to return to her station (at Nyakach)," Elwood states in one of his letters.

There was a movement in the mid-1920s among the mission bodies that saw revival among themselves and confession and repentance over wrong feelings and attitudes held toward each other and their African friends. Conferences were held annually to 'fan the flame' of this renewal movement. The Kikuyu people, especially the women, benefited from the missions' united stand; both spiritually and in practical policies like the opposition to female circumcision.

Floyd and Betty Pearson, missionary friends, pass through Kenya on their way to Congo.

As they began their second furlough on April 15, 1925, aboard the *SS Gloucester Castle* Elwood wrote, "It was hard leaving a place where we seemed needed so much and where we were wanted. If the Lord tarries, maybe we will return better equipped to serve him wherever He sees we can best serve Him." They did return in 1926 and enjoyed a fruitful ministry for the next 23 years.

A small but significant incident occurred in 1928 when Gideon and Rosie Mwangi gave Elwood and Bernice a turkey for Christmas dinner. They were active members of the Kijabe AIC and Gideon was an elder. (This was like the Macedonian believers helping the Apostle Paul.)

On a Saturday night in October 1932, the missionaries heard the Royal Train—carrying the Prince of Wales—was to pass through

Kijabe Station at 8.30 pm. As it was to make a brief stop there, some of the missionaries went to the station. Elwood was too busy at the hospital to go, so Bernice went down to the station with several other missionaries. When the Prince exited the train he asked each missionary his or her name, where they were from and how long they had been in Kenya and then he shook each of their hands. Those missionaries who met the Prince besides Bernice were Mrs. Propst, Roxanna, Mrs. Sokim from India, Marjorie Bryson from Australia, Miss Slater and Miss Perrott from England, Miss Moody from Winnipeg, Canada, and Miss Stephenson from Chicago.

Since Bernice was fluent in the local Kikuyu language, she interpreted for the Prince as he spoke with the Africans gathered there. "He was perfectly free and natural and laughed and joked," Bernice wrote to her son Linnell. "He told us not to tell the American newspapers all he had said. I told him he has as much privacy as a goldfish." But she was so obedient to his wish that she did not even record what the Prince had said in the detailed letters she wrote.

The Rift Valley Academy (RVA) orchestra, on the Kiambogo porch in the 1920s. From right to left: Jim Propst, Charles Propst, Philip Davis, possibly Bernice Dalziel, the next two are unidentified.

At the height of the busy schedule in medical work and the tensions related to the activities of the Kikuyu Central Association, a natural phenomenon occurred. "An earthquake in January 1928 caused Lake Naivasha to recede ½ of a mile." (This happened literally overnight!)

"On May 7, 1929, we took a train to Kisumu to spend a month's holiday at Kaimosi." (More often than not, though, vacations were often filled with ministries and visits with people.) "In our compartment Bernice got a bedbug on her coat so we told the station master at Nakuru. He (kindly) put us in first class the rest of the way to Kisumu. Mr. Bond met us and we had breakfast at the station restaurant. The cook was Mr. Coralis who used to be the head cook at the Kijabe Station Hotel. He had made the Kijabe Station Hotel famous with his cooking.

"We went to visit Mr. Keller's mission at Nyang'ori (Pentecostal Assemblies of Canada). (Mr. Keller was the father of famous Christian author Philip Keller.) From Kellers we went to Miss Bolt's (Church of God) Mission at Kima. We met Dr. and Mrs. Henderson there. Then we finally arrived at Dr. Bolt's mission at Kaimosi and spent a month.

"But during our time there we had some safaris, too. The first Sunday we went to an outreach of the mission and attended church there. The next week we went on a long safari to Nyakach with Dr. Bond. The Inneses, Gladys Clarke and Dr. and Mrs. Green are posted there. I had a long talk with Dr. Green about mission matters.

"The next day we drove to Litein and back (also a long safari in a Model T Ford of Mr. Innes). On the way back we had no lights so we had to tie a lantern on the front. I also used my flashlight to help.

"We left Dr. Bond's on April 1 as I had to return to testify in a police case. We helped pay for Dr. Bond's car to take us home. We stopped at Kapsabet where the Brysons and Miss Boyce are and at Ravine where the Albert Barnetts have been. We passed through two miles of locusts" (after leaving Ravine).

"On June 29, a Fuller Brush man drove into Kijabe. We bought a few things from him. Later that day an Indian was brought in with part of his foot blown off from his gun trap that went off as he was setting the trap for a leopard."

In August 1929 Elwood writes, "We went to the same spot where the Davis family and Stauffachers spent a week camping in 1921 on the banks of the Narok River" (about 20 miles west of Narok town.) On the way to camp Elwood writes, "We stopped to see a man drilling for water on Mt. Margaret Estate. He had reached 620 feet but still no water. The temperature in the well had gone from 97º to 120º Fahrenheit. They were still going deeper and all through volcanic soil.

"In September we went by the drill site again and found they were at 713 feet, the deepest known well in Kenya, and still no water. But on September 10 Mr. Andersen told me they had struck water at 720 feet and had drilled to a total of 750 feet. They were getting 300 gallons of water per hour."

Mr. Andersen also told them that warthogs were such a nuisance that he paid the local Maasai one shilling for every pig tail they brought to him. Within a couple days they had bought 70 tails. So then he offered them two shillings for every tail and again within a couple days they had brought him 120 tails.

Mountain climbing in the Rift Valley around Kijabe was a great diversion from the work. Elwood wrote that during one mission conference some missionary men climbed Mt. Longonot and went down into the crater. Those in the group were Dr. Green, Mr. Teasdale, Mr. Pitway (the conference speaker), Mr. Borkham, Mr. Beules and Elwood. They found the crater to be very rough, hard volcanic stone, uneven and pitted in odd ways.

That same month Henry Senff, missionary to Congo, took a mule from Kijabe to Longonot leaving the mule at the station and climbing to the rim of the crater. He then went down inside and crossed the crater floor, using the directions given him by Elwood. Later that month Senff joined John Stauffacher—renowned for his many climbs up the Ruwenzori Mountains in Congo—and Elwood climbed nearby Suswa Mountain.

Elwood notes, "There is a peak in the middle with a deep chasm all around it. It is called 'no man's land' as no one has ever crossed it. So

Henry said he wanted to try it. He went down the steep chasm and up to the peak. We walked around the other side to wait for him. Henry found that when he came to the summit of the hill that was inside the crater he could go no farther. There was a lot of soft mud with steam jets coming out of it. It was reddish in color. He went back the way he had come and came around to meet us on the other side."

Elwood writes on December 23, 1929, that Dr. Green from Nyakach went on furlough so once again he was the only doctor in the AIM in Kenya.

Elwood (centre) and Bernice (right) with Nurse Stevenson and trainees on the steps of the Theodora Hospital at Kijabe in the 1920s.

That Christmas they dined on a turkey given by Mrs. Dalziel, along with mashed potatoes, gravy, peas, jelly, spiced figs, salad, nuts, mince pie, cheese, coffee and candy.

In the late 1920s and early 1930s there was a very powerful insidious movement to return the Kikuyu people to their old cultural customs, the primary one being the circumcision of girls to prepare them for marriage. Some of these practices included drinking blood, taking oaths, and sexual acts. Some missionaries received death threats. Grandpa Davis was handed a letter by one of the workers at the hospital telling him that his services were no longer needed and he should leave. Church attendance dwindled from 700 down to 30. The girls' school of over 300 girls decreased to 80. Natives from the forbidden movement called the Kikuyu Central Association (KCA) threw stones at the dormitories and mission houses at Kijabe. When missionaries took young people from Kijabe to other churches, the young Kikuyu believers were threatened and mocked. There was a threat of an uprising on Christmas Day 1929, so for the first time ever Elwood and Bernice (and others) locked their doors!

A big issue was the refusal of all mission societies to allow female circumcision (now called female genital mutilation or FGM). The KCA made this the uniting issue to their people. The movement gained tremendous momentum and they even started their own schools, harassing young people in the mission schools.

Bernice Davis and Kikuyu ladies listening to a gramophone at Kijabe in the 1920s.

The Rev. Lee Downing was the leader of AIM in Kenya at the time. He was fluent in Kikuyu and his leadership and courage sustained the fearful mission family during these troubling days.

One single female missionary told Bernice she was so afraid she wanted to leave. "I felt like crying, too," records Bernice in a letter to her sons, far away and safe in the United States. Linnell had remained in the states when Elwood and Bernice returned to Kenya in 1926 at the end of their second furlough. Philip did the same after their next furlough.

It surely was one of the darkest hours in AIM history when Miss Hulda Stumpf, the principal of Kijabe Girls' School, was murdered in her bed on the night of January 2, 1930. On February 12, 1930, Bernice went to Kiambu, where the government administrative offices were located, with Dr. Blakeslee and Miss Stumpf's native boy. Captain Cochran, Superintendent of Police, was there and took their testimony. A Mr. Griffin from CID (Criminal Investigation Department) had come to the station earlier.

Lee Downing and the missionaries decided to make clear who was on their side in this battle against the darkness of evil. They asked all their staff, students and professing believers to sign a letter saying they opposed FGM. Most signed. Some left. But this brought a new wave of persecution from the KCA.

The AIM Kijabe Church in 1920.

In their letters, Elwood and Bernice give some details of the situation at the time. "The Association has much money so it may be likely to do anything to secure their evil ends. One boy went to Nairobi and heard all the songs and speeches by the Association; he was horrified and came back and told folk at the Scottish Mission at Kikuyu he was ready to sign with them because he did not want to be part of the crowd in Nairobi.

"It does seem this is a testing time of the church and even worse things may happen. Nyakiru, wife of the late Njuguna Wamanyira, a couple who had been Christians for 20 years and even went to Congo with Charles Hurlburt, was the leader of the heathen circumcision dances. The Association people taunt the Christians when they go home. They tell them that the mission will have to baptize baboons as there will be no more natives to baptize. So you can see evil is abroad and no one knows what will come next. But we do know God is watching over us. He is stronger than all the forces of evil and nothing can happen to me that He does not allow."

When boys went to their homes upcountry or to Nairobi, they found they were 'known' by the KCA network. They would be refused work, food, transport or any kindness. Instead, they were mocked and ridiculed. Sometimes the food they had brought to eat was thrown on the ground.

"On February 17," writes Elwood, "I went to Nairobi to the Alliance meetings. The next day I stayed with Canon Burns, as his place was closer to where the meetings were held. I was elected treasurer of the KMA (Kenya Missionary Association); this was besides having responsibility for four other funds.

"There were some interesting meetings, especially concerning the circumcision situation and we took strong action against it and were practically all of one mind in the face of disagreements of some government officials. We see the great harm it has done to the church, which is and must be our chief concern."

Elwood writes of a later incident: "One of the prominent men against the mission became very sick and was brought to the mission. After nine days he was better and when he went home there was a positive change toward the mission."

There is no doubt the Christians and missionaries suffered during this period. Some years later, Mr. Bingham, Director of Sudan Interior Mission (SIM) said, "Suffering would be at a premium in Heaven. People would see how well it is rewarded and be willing to come back to earth again to suffer for Jesus' sake in order to receive what will be given to those who have suffered for Him."

The first Machakos church with AIM Missionary Fred McKenrick in the 1920s. McKenrick was the father of Florene who became the Davis boys' Aunt Florene Eddings.

Elwood notes, "As the hospital boys have not signed the papers against female circumcision we decided they were not in the right spiritual condition to continue conducting prayers in the hospital. So we three do the devotions.

"On the first Sunday three confessed Christ as Savior and two signed the paper against circumcision and later two others asked what more they could do for Jesus as they wanted to serve Him in everything. A dozen girls stood up to confess Christ."

The murder of Miss Stumpf and the failure of the police to charge anyone with the murder had brought the missionary community to a low point. Most had served together for 10 or 20 years. But within a year the tenacious band of mature missionaries saw their faithfulness rewarded. Church membership climbed to over 1,000 at Kijabe. The girls' school enrolled nearly 800 girls. Probably most significant, the Kikuyu Central Association lost much of its support as the major mission societies united to reject the female circumcision rites and other pagan practices of the society.

The missionaries enjoyed interesting and more light-hearted experiences as tensions eased. Elwood and Bernice often went to Siyapei Mission Station in Maasailand to visit their good friends the John Stauffachers. They would shoot game on the way, camp overnight, go hunting and fishing and enjoy being away from the demands of Kijabe Hospital and mission station responsibilities. My Dad, Linnell, remembered that in 1923 when he was 10 years old it took three days by ox cart to go from RVA at Kijabe to Siyapei in Maasai country—a distance of 70 miles. They shot their own meat—often gazelle or guinea fowl along the way—and listened to the sounds of lion, hyenas and jackals every night.

Dr. Elwood Davis (right) with Roy Shaffer Senior and a visitor on safari in Maasai country in the 1920s.

From Foot Safaris to Helicopters

From right to left: John and Florence Stauffacher, Elwood and Bernice Davis and their son Philip at Siyapei in the 1920s.

Grandma and Grandpa never owned a car in their nearly 40 years in Africa, so they always depended on others for transport. Sometimes they rode with other missionaries or lorry drivers going their way. Many times they traveled by train as it had regular passenger service upcountry and to the coast.

A note from Elwood's diary tells more of the vagaries of travel in those days: "Took Norman Johnsons to train, but Mr. Propst's truck stuck in mud, had to walk to station. Late for train. Waited a couple hours for goods train. Caught up to passenger train at Kabete. Got into Nairobi in time to shop and take another train home. The new people (like Johnsons) wondered why they have to experience such difficulties. So we tell them that is the way of Africa conditions, which are uncertain and unusual."

Those early days of travel by oxcart or mule were slow and relaxing, but also rough trips. On one oxcart ride up the Kilungu Hills, Elwood counted 103 curves in the road. Noting details was his specialty! But as the hospital became busier and more vehicles came into the country, car or lorry was the way to go!

On one memorable trip to Siyapei, Elwood and Bernice got a ride with an Asian shopkeeper in his lorry. When the lorry was seriously delayed, they thought of transferring to the post office lorry, but didn't. Later in the afternoon, when they were halfway to Siyapei, they saw the post office lorry broken down so were glad they weren't on it.

Elwood writes of a trip to Subukia to visit Captain Ney, a farmer, and to hold church services for the Europeans and the farm workers. They traveled north to Nakuru, drove by the Menengai Crater down into the Solai Valley, over a range of hills, seeing Lake Baringo and Marmanet at 8,565 feet, the highest point on the Laikipia Plateau. He gave the message at the Kikuyu service in the chapel on the farm. Many Kikuyu from nearby farms came to the service. Mr. Farnsworth preached at the European service held in one of their homes and 25 attended.

One of the main reasons they did not own a car was that it simply was too expensive to buy and maintain one. For most of their years of service, financial support was below the needed level to adequately cover living expenses, so Grandpa records that from time to time he would shoot jackals and would get three shillings for a pelt. That was a good amount of money in those days. On another occasion a kind and considerate fellow missionary, Lee Downing, gave them a gift of 100 shillings so they could have a two-week holiday in the AIM mission guesthouse in Nairobi.

Elwood and Bernice at the Kikuyu guesthouse with Canon Burns in the 1920s.

Many missionaries were under-supported and would shoot game animals to fill their larders with meat so they would have money to buy other necessities. Fred McKenrick, our Aunt Florene's Dad, would regularly walk down to the plains below Kijabe and shoot antelope, or go above Kijabe to shoot giant forest hogs. One forest hog he shot weighed 610 pounds!

Elwood, Linnell and Philip on a hunting safari in the Kedong Valley in about 1923.

The work load and responsibilities were heavy and missionaries went for long times without a break. They were a hardy lot in those days. "I am just looking forward to the time when I can take a train to Mombasa and just rest, rest, rest," says Elwood in a letter.

But God faithfully encouraged and rewarded those in medical work. This letter was one of those times:

"It Wasn't Like Dying"

A native woman, one of our former patients, returned to dispensary one day and was asked about her little girl. We were told that she had returned home, she had gone to her owner. When she saw that we did not understand, she said that the child died shortly after returning home from the hospital. Then very quickly she said: "It wasn't like dying and we don't feel badly. She slept away after telling us things which caused us such astonishment and wonder."

She was ill only two days and during that time did not seem very sick. When asked how she felt, she said: "I don't feel badly, but I am thinking."

The mother asked her of what she was thinking. She answered: "I want to know if you know where the wind comes from and where it goes to."

The mother replied, "No".

"Well, I know," continued the child, "so I am wiser than you."

She then told the mother that Jesus died for her and repeated John 3:16, "For God so loved the world, that he gave his only begotten son, that whosoever believeth in him should not perish, but have everlasting life."

The mother wanted to know where she had learned that. The child said she had been taught it at Theodora Hospital. The mother called in the father. She realized that the Holy Spirit was speaking through the child. She repeated the verse for the child's father. He then called in the neighbors and told them his child had good words to tell them. When the people had gathered, she told them of God's love and sang the chorus, "Jesus loves the little children," which too she had been taught at the hospital.

The people left and the child asked her mother for a clean dress. She was asked to wait until the next day, but replied: "No, I want a clean dress now. I don't know when Jesus will come and where he is nothing is dirty."

The mother put a clean dress on the child and then laid her down and covered her up, as she wanted to go to sleep. A little later they turned down the covers to see how she was, and found that she had gone to be with the Lord.

"But it wasn't like dying, it was just as if she had returned to her owner," the mother said, "and now we want to be strong in the things of God and we have no doubt that some day we shall see her again. We do rejoice much because of the words she left with us."

Jesus said, "Of such is the kingdom of heaven."

During the early years transport was done on foot with porters carrying the loads, by ox cart or by mule back. The completion of the railway line, or 'iron snake' as Africans named it, was a major improvement. But travel was still tedious, filled with the unexpected, and took a long time.

CHAPTER 3

Life in the Roaring Twenties and Thirties

The personal feelings of missionaries affect their relationship to the people to whom they minister. Bernice was always very candid and forthright. On January 30, 1930, she sadly wrote to Linnell: "I personally feel like the night has come when no man can work. Unless God's Holy Spirit works in their hearts we might as well let them alone. I don't feel like wasting my time on them if they don't want the Gospel . . . I can't conceive what would make them (so) antagonistic after all the missionaries have done for them all these years—except that Satan has entered their hearts."

Family letters reveal interesting aspects of life at Kijabe during those days: The Davises kept dairy cows and report that they were giving 16 quarts of milk a day. After one cow heifered they were getting 20 quarts of milk a day and sharing the extra with other missionaries and patients at the hospital. There was lots of rain and Elwood supervised the planting of hundreds of tree seedlings below the hospital. (Elwood's great grandson Jeffrey Davis, now living at Kijabe with his family, is active in tree planting as well.)

The heavy rains in 1930 washed out roads and bridges. The Teasdale family took three-and-a-half days to travel by car from Nairobi to Mulango, a distance of 120 miles.

During the months of April and May, the Kijabe area received over 20 inches of rain. When Elwood checked the water level in a dam near the first ravine, he heard a great roaring sound—not animals, he noted, but flowing high water. The next day there was a gap 48 feet wide and five feet deep in the road and they were cut off from the outside world until the old road to the train station was opened.

An unusual sight was also seen during that rainy season: a rainbow by the light of the moon.

Often their medical work took them away from the hospital to see others with medical needs: at Kijabe railway station Elwood treated Goanese patients; at Mt. Margaret Estate he treated a Mr. Andersen, who owned the farm. A variety of patients came to the hospital as well: patients in the Asiatic ward, including a Goanese from Narok and an Indian with a broken leg, who had previously shot himself in the foot. Another Indian had been mauled by a leopard.

The students at Rift Valley Academy also needed care. Dr Davis reported that two-thirds of the students at RVA got sick on bad tinned salmon.

The controversy over female circumcision continued into the 1930s. Elwood writes on May 10, 1930: "On Sunday there were 30 children in Sunday School and 65 in church. Mr. Lee Downing gave them a strong message in Kikuyu (at Siyapei). Mulingit (a church elder) and other Maasai of the opposition were there and at the close of the service asked the same old tiring questions.

"The following day, Monday, a number of elders and leaders in the opposition came to have a talk with John Stauffacher, Lee Downing and myself. The missionaries felt they were obstinate and determined in their way and gave such poor excuses for continuing in their old ways.

"For three Sundays someone went to Matathia to hold meetings to see if people there really wanted the church services to continue. The Sunday Mr. Teasdale went, 12 people came. Some boys picked flowers to take back to Mrs. Teasdale and the people (those opposed to the teaching) complained that they destroyed the flower patch.

"The second Sunday Dr. Blakeslee and Miss Collins went and only one boy went along. The local (opposition) people said bad things about him. Three boys and two girls were there. One boy prayed and talked about shaking the dust off their feet if the witnesses of Jesus are not wanted. Later, people on the outside who had heard the boy's prayer said mean things to him. The third Sunday Mr. Teasdale and two boys went and no one came to that service."

An encouragement was that on April 20, 1930, Easter, three boys and four girls were baptized at Kijabe Chapel. They all signed the card against female circumcision. They had been in class for two years. At Kikuyu, 20 people were baptized and some others stood up to show they were against female circumcision.

When Stauffachers went back to Siyapei from conference they had a meeting with the Christians about female circumcision. To their surprise all but two went against the mission stand, even Mulingit. Matters were taken to the District Commissioner whom the missionaries felt was not at all helpful. But Mulingit's wife came and told Mr. Stauffacher that some of the people were tired of the elders holding out, and so they were going to return to church.

A new policeman, Mr. Peacock, was assigned to investigate the murder of Miss Stumpf and that seemed to bring new evidence to light. A boy named Karanja was the last one to see the suspect, but he disappeared.

Not all of missionary life was spent coping with the spiritual and physical battles against heathen practices. Missionaries and their kids wisely made time for fun and for holidays.

During one school holiday Philip (their second son) and Alec Anderson walked all the way out first ravine to Mr. Andersen's ranch (a distance of six miles) and he brought them back by car. Philip also enjoyed shooting parrots. (In the next generation, Linnell's sons Van and Art also shot green parrots and Van became infected with green parrot fever.)

The Davis family went for a long overdue holiday and stayed at Kikuyu where they played tennis every day. Elwood was happy to sleep in and have his Postum, bread and butter in bed! In the afternoon they went to tea with Dr. and Mrs. Arthur, Presbyterian missionaries at Kikuyu.

On other occasions they would go to the Coast for holidays, sometimes staying at the Church Mission Society guesthouse in

Mombasa. Elwood's letter gives the following details: "We arrived here on July 1. Mr. Downing met us at the train station and took us across the ferry to the guesthouse. On the ferry, passengers pay six cents and cars two shillings each. They also have a rowboat people can take across. We have a cool ocean breeze here. We are in a large three-room house (but we use only one room) with 18-inch walls, high ceilings and corrugated iron roof, four windows on the sea side, a door and a window on the land side. We have fruit and fish every day. The most common fish is *chungu,* and *chafu,* a black fish. We didn't bring a worker with us this time, but are doing all the work ourselves. The CMS (Church Mission Society) has given up their work here and have moved all European missionaries out. The buildings are to be rented out. The natives are in charge of the church work.

"Boats (ocean going ships) come and go every day and we buy a newspaper to keep track of them. I would so love to get on a boat and travel as I do like boat travel and change of scenery. I have no desire to leave my work, but just to enjoy traveling.

"An Indian, Dhala Ismail, whom we knew when we first went to Machakos in 1911, came to see us one day and took us over in his car to their place. They have four rooms on the ground floor of a three-story building and he pays 125 shillings per month rent. We were given tea at the house, then lunch for three shillings and fifty cents at the Palace Hotel. He paid all our expenses besides giving us fish and nuts, fruit and lettuce. I examined his wife and son and prescribed medicines for them.

"A native man whom we also knew at Machakos is here working in the PC's office. His son took us to see Matthew Wellington, who traveled with David Livingstone. Matthew, born in Malawi, was sold as a slave when young, but was rescued by a British warship and taken first to India where he learned the art of embalming, then later to Zanzibar, where he was trained by the CMS. He became a Christian on Zanzibar and from there was chosen by David Livingstone to be his porter guide.

Matthew Wellington in Mombasa in 1932. He was among the group that carried David Livingstone's body to Bagamoyo.

"He lives a mile from us. He is 89 and quite old and feeble. He has made a living raising and selling pineapples. His daughter lives in a good-sized white house near us and was married to an American who had come out as an engineer on a boat. We talked with Matthew, who speaks fairly good English. Mama took his picture. He also knew Henry Stanley. He is the last living person to have known Stanley and Livingstone."

Later, Elwood learned more of the story. Wellington was one of the party of 80 who brought Livingstone's body to the coast from the interior at Rifiji. They removed the internal organs, packed his body in salt, folded up the legs, and carried the body in bark so it would not be seen by the people they passed by, as some were superstitious about carrying dead bodies. It took them nine months to reach the coast. Elwood learned that Matthew had been living in Mombasa since his arrival in 1874 at 33 years of age. When he first came to live in Mombasa, he saw lions near his place. Now at 89 he still walked a mile to church every Sunday.

"The people here are mainly Wanyika though there are also Kamba and Kikuyu here. The Swahili women dress in a 'showy' manner but always have their black cloths covering their other clothes. The Swahili men wear white and appear very 'haughty' and independent.

"Philip went riding on Mr. Jensen's motorcycle. August 1 we went over to Jensens to examine their daughter who has had headaches for many years. Mrs. Jensen treated us to the Mombasa Club for lunch today. Jensens take care of the CMS home. They are Danish. On July 28 I visited Mr. Jensen's 150 acre farm four miles away."

Mr. Jensen took Elwood on the back of his motorcycle to see the farm. Of course Elwood noted some details: "He has neat rows of coconut palms, each row 25 feet away from the next. Each tree bears about 40 nuts a year and after 18 years bears fruit year round. He only gets 4 cents a nut (current price is 10 shillings each) and produces about 200,000 a year."

Elwood noted that they go to the Coast in June, July, or August because rail fares are half price and it was also the cool season. They enjoyed walking along the road on the edge of the ocean, going by government buildings, Fort Jesus, a lighthouse, and old relics of Portuguese forts. As they were walking one day, they saw the Governor, His Excellency, Sir Edward Grigg, go by in a motor car.

Birdlife was plentiful with different varieties from the highlands of Kijabe. One seemed to say, 'Zebediah, Zebediah, Zebediah,' repeatedly. Another said, 'Hurry home, hurry home.'

"Early on July 25, 1930, a German warship, the cruiser *Karlshrue*, came into port. The English cruiser, already in port, fired a 21 gun salute."

"In Mombasa at this time (July 1930) there are 26,000 natives, 7,000 Arabs, 21,000 Indians and 1,300 Europeans."

Back at Kijabe after their holiday, life continued at its hectic pace. At the end of August 1930 there was a 21st 'birthday of RVA' celebration with students providing the entertainment and Mr. Downing and Mr. Propst giving some history. All former students' names were mentioned and prayed for.

One day Elwood had lunch with McKenricks and then went with them to Githumu where a plague had broken out. While there he gave serum injections and checked Mr. McKenrick's symptoms of back pain. (Later, Cedric Eddings—my mother's brother—married Florene, one of the McKenrick daughters. Cedric and Florene Eddings, my uncle and aunt, served as missionaries in Venezuela.)

Church matters became more encouraging as on August 30, 1930, the wife and daughter of John Nyenjeri (the late and greatly loved Pastor Yohana of Kijabe) came forward after holding out for a long time. Then the wife of a Maasai, Ndilai, another Bible school student, took a stand for Christ.

"A Maasai girl who had been here from January to August finally made a stand for Christ and went home. But she turned against spiritual things causing the missionaries to wonder if her father threatened her."

The investigation into the murder of Miss Stumpf continued and, "Finally, on October 9, 1930, the case of the native accused of killing Miss Stumpf began. He did not seem interested until the matter of the manner she was killed came up. Then he seemed very interested (as if to see if they had deducted how he did it). He said some funny things like it 'was a European' who told him to do it."

Medical work called Elwood again to Narok—two times in two weeks to see a Goanese woman. The second time he slept on a camp cot that had been recently used by an Italian Count when the 'white hunter' Mr. Lucy came to be treated for lion wounds. On his return trip he shot a jackal and the following week sold the hide for 3 shillings which helped buy more shotgun shells.

Visits with fellow missionaries continued. Mr. and Mrs. Kellum of the Friends Mission from Kaimosi came by and were persuaded to go home via Siyapei, as one bridge had washed out. Elwood and Philip went with them to show the way, allowing Philip to shoot a jackal and a rabbit and on the way back a couple partridges.

They heard a Maasai man was to come in a car and take one of the Christian Maasai girls by force to marry her. For her own protection Elwood and Bernice locked her in the hospital. The car came, but it left when they didn't find the girl.

Responsibilities were many and important. At conference in January 1931 Elwood was elected to the school board, then asked to be president of the board. Also, as chairman of the station committee, he had to collect three shillings from every missionary each month to pay for roads and maintenance. Part of his job at the hospital also entailed overseeing the ongoing building. He would go down to first ravine to confirm the measurement of stone for the second floor of the hospital.

Much time was spent in prayer, too, by these hardy missionaries. They had departmental prayer times and station prayer times, besides long times of personal prayer every morning and evening. "Prayer is the great power at present to do the work we want to see accomplished," Elwood wrote. The need and urgency for prayer was often intensified by serious circumstances that led to human suffering that overpowered their resources and efforts.

On April 10 Bernice wrote, "A native woman said that she did not agree with the others when they were considering killing Mr. and Mrs. Lee Downing. She had been one of us, but had gone out from us. Then she felt compelled to come back and talk to the Downings about the threats."

Just a month after these threats on his life, Lee Downing expressed a deep and powerful sense of God's power and sovereignty in the death of a teenage boy. "It was worth coming to Africa to see such a victorious death," Bernice wrote of Lee's response to the boy's death. "Henry had been unwell for years, having had a bad heart. He woke at 9 pm with abdominal pain and cried out and wanted to be held with pressure on his abdomen. He had a high fever. His father held him. He sang hymns and said John 3:16. When his father asked if he was saved, he said he was and that he was now going to God. He spat out pus and blood and said he was going to die. He called for his mother and told her he was going to die. He asked her to leave greetings for all the children and his playmates."

Lee Downing's words were echoed by all the missionaries at Kijabe and they knew all their efforts were well worthwhile to see a native die so victoriously and with such confidence in his salvation and assurance of going to see God.

The efforts continued with renewed intensity and this even despite increased opposition. "The first Sunday of April (1931) six boys and one girl were baptized. <u>And this means a public stand against evil customs</u> (such as female circumcision). In the evening seven more stood up to publicly confess Christ. The next Sunday four more stood up."

That same Sunday Lawson Propst and Welles Devitt went to preach at Kinino (Kinale today) and there were 42 in the service. The KCA (Kikuyu Central Association) heard of it and would not let the missionaries come back the next Sunday.

"At Kijabe during this time men came out of the forest every night and made loud noises and threw stones at the girls' school and the missionary houses. Miss Gruenvald (unperturbed) went out when these men came and shot her gun into the air. The government has sent two Kikuyu spies to find out who these night raiders are.

"On July 18, after delivering the station master's wife of a child, we returned in Mr. Farnsworth's car to the hospital. A native met us at the hospital and handed us a note. The note said, "Your services are not needed anymore, and all is over with" (a thinly veiled death threat to Elwood and Bernice).

At the same time, the church was growing. "The first Sunday in July, 21 stood up to confess Christ. We had had a special prayer meeting on the afternoon of the 20th to pray for revival throughout the colony. This was done at the request of believers from another mission. Since then, there have been wonderful manifestations of God's protecting care. For example, God has protected our mission stations and out-schools from the locust plague." On November 9, 1931, Elwood wrote that he "killed 500 locusts and Mr. Devitt killed 200. On October 10 I killed 1,000 locusts before 7 am."

"Mr. Flinn left our mission years ago, but he is still serving the Lord," Elwood writes in a letter to Linnell, reminding him that Mr. Flinn was the one who took care of him sometimes when they were at Mombasa when Linnell was a child. "Mr. and Mrs. Flinn are now with the CMS in Tanzania. Mr. Flinn is the one that told us about the Maasai fable of the rope to God. Flinn said this rope hung down to Suswa Mountain. When people pulled on it, God appeared and listened to their requests. God would then send down things by the rope. One day someone pulled too hard and the rope broke. Since then no more blessings have come down."

There was still opposition to the strong stand held by the missionaries. "The natives of Githumu wanted to have their schools go under CMS because they are not so strict on tobacco use, liquor and traditional practices. And the troublesome KCA want all Europeans out and to have control of everything and that would be a disaster," writes Elwood. "A critical situation has arisen in the work in Githumu District. A report has been sent to me that caused me to write 11 letters at once." (He does not say what it's about, but no doubt had to do with the Kikuyu Central Association and female circumcision.)

"God is with us," writes Elwood, "and we do not fear, but it means no compromise with the forces of evil and we will undoubtedly feel the effects as a result of our determined stand for what is right. Two other missions are standing with us. The elders met me later and told me some things about female circumcision and Kikuyu customs that had made them want to have nothing to do with it and want to keep their children from it."

He notes in his dairy, "I found that the Agikuyu customs were more rotten than I used to think. Now I can sympathize more fully with the native Christians than ever before and may be able to write up something that will help other missionaries to better understand the standpoint of those who are fighting this evil custom so determinedly."

In those roaring adventurous days of the 1920s and 1930s Kenya was the wilderness playground for many Europeans and Americans. Lords, dukes, film stars, the Prince of Wales and millionaires all found their way to East Africa to collect great trophies of elephant, rhino, lion and buffalo. Many went just to enjoy the dangerous and exciting wilds of 'Darkest Africa'. Martin and Osa Johnson, noted for their photography, viewed the game from their personal zebra-striped biplane.

Many bought houses and lands, even huge ranches. The 'Happy Valley' stories came from those 'morally loose' Europeans who were away from their homes, their restrictive ethics and the socially binding rules of a Christianized Europe and America.

One day in 1932, Dr. Davis was working his rounds at the Kijabe Hospital when a dashing new red car drove up to the entrance of the hospital. A European man jumped out in a great fit of anxiety and asked Elwood to please come with him to save his wife's life.

As they raced off on the rough dusty road—sometimes at 60 mph in the newest model of a Buick—he saw some pieces of mail on the seat of the car next to him. The mail was addressed to Lord Erroll. Elwood realized he was riding with a member of the House of Lords, an Earl by the name of the Right Honorable Earl of Erroll. Dr. Elwood did save the life of Lord Erroll's wife, a Countess. They were so grateful that the following week the Earl and Countess of Erroll picked Elwood and Bernice up at Kijabe and took them to their home—the Djinn Palace at Oserian on the south shores of Lake Naivasha—for the night.

Dr. Elwood Davis was called by Lord Erroll to treat his wife Mary at their Oserian farm on Lake Naivasha where this photo was taken. From left to right: The Honorable Michael Kinross, possibly Ben Birkbeck, Lord Erroll, Dr. Elwood Davis, Mary Countess of Erroll and Cockie Birkbeck. Photo taken in 1932.

Later Bernice writes to Linnell, "I was just interrupted by the Earl and Countess coming to stay for lunch. Papa called last Sunday to see her. She was quite ill. (Today) they brought us six lovely fresh fish and gave Papa a check for 200 shillings" (a sizeable sum then).

When they arrived at Oserian for that first visit, they noted that the Countess had been fixing up the grounds, planting Kikuyu grass and putting flowers in a rock garden. Unexpectedly, they met other guests there, the younger sons of a Lord who were having a trip through Africa with their mother, Lady Balfour. "The men drank and played cards most of the night," Grandma noted. "But the Errolls turned in early and were a really nice couple," she added. The other guests left the next morning and then the Lord and Countess showed Elwood and Bernice around their 7,000 acre ranch, after being served breakfast in bed! They also saw the Errolls' valuable works of art.

"The great question in our minds is why the Lord God had them come into our lives. Pray that we may minister to their souls, not just their bodies," Bernice wrote to Linnell. So no doubt Elwood and Bernice talked to them about eternal matters as well. As missionaries, they not only came to Africa to tell the native peoples that *it is really true*—that Jesus is God, died to pay for their sins and promises eternal life to any who will believe in Him—but also the European and Asian peoples.

From Elwood and Bernice's letters to their sons, we get a flavor of their rich, mixed, and ever-changing daily programs.

On January 16, 1932, Bernice writes, "Evelyn Camp of Congo came through." Just in that one phrase alone lays a whole chapter of daily life activities. If Evelyn could tell her story of adventures along the way we would no doubt hear of delays, breakdown of the car, border crossing traumas, food eaten, overnight lodging, being stuck in the mud, wild animal stories and many more.

In the same letter she writes, "Mr. Farnsworth brought the Saums from Nairobi. McKenricks moved back to their house. That same evening we had a visit by Hans Von Staden of the African Evangelistic Band of South Africa. Mr. Von Staden went to the 300 South Africans in Tanzania and he is now visiting the thousands of South Africans in Kenya." A vivid imagination could not capture the myriad of stories that Von Staden must have passed on to Elwood and Bernice that evening.

The whole purpose of Elwood and Bernice's stay in Africa was for the church, and to serve Jesus Christ, their Savior and God. Much of their correspondence relates to what was happening in the church.

On March 12, 1932 Bernice writes, "There are encouraging developments in the church. The first Sunday of February five people confessed Christ, 10 the second Sunday, 24 the third Sunday. Two men were licensed to preach this month in Kijabe area and two more for Machakos area. The church membership at Kijabe had been 700 before the troubles of 1929 and 1930, and then went down to 30. Now it is up to 1,300."

Things were so bad financially on the mission field as a result of the depression in the US that a special prayer meeting was called for. "On February 6 we had special prayer for the financial needs of the mission. The (very) next day we got word from Mr. Campbell (of the US office) that all of us would get 100% of our support for the previous December. Then we got a gift of $40 to be divided among the missionaries." (This was a big gift in those days. It probably came to about $5 per couple, equal to $500 today.)

On another 'un-average' day, Elwood writes, "I was put on a committee to welcome Indian evangelists who were coming to evangelize their own people. I was also asked to be on the board of governors of Alliance High School."

One other time, "We went with Mr. Reynolds to inspect schools. We were in an open box body Ford with no windshield on my side and mud was splattering all over us. We went to Matara where there are no missionaries at present. We visited an outschool near there first and then decided to sell some boards from one of the mission buildings as it was getting pretty dilapidated."

From the days Mr. Reynolds worked at an outschool in Kinyoo he told of a time of famine that was very severe in the area. But God provided more blackberries on the bushes than ever before. There were also more partridges than ever so people had enough to eat even in the famine.

On July 18 Elwood wrote, "Five of us went to the Falls for a picnic with four visiting single missionary men from Greece and Crete.

"The next day, Sunday, we had the four men for lunch. That afternoon I had to treat Lee Downing, who had done a baptism in the morning and was feeling chilled. He is no longer a young man (60s) and has to be more careful. That evening I attended field council meetings.

"A few days later we went (up the hill) to Kenton College to attend Keswick meetings. And the following month Bernice went to Kikinobuiri (Mr. Knapp's station) to attend a native conference. There were over 3,000 people there."

Another time Elwood treated a patient who was a friend of Mrs. Picksford. They were then invited to the Picksford home, set on a hill five miles northeast of Naivasha. Another guest was Colonel Henderson who owned a farm on the Kinangop Plateau. Elwood accompanied the Colonel as he played a round of golf on the course laid out on what was formerly the bed of Lake Naivasha (before the earthquake changed things). Mrs. Picksford was the sister of Lord Balfour, of the Balfour Declaration, a proposal to set up the independent state of Israel.

Bernice was in charge of the Kikuyu language teaching and exams for Miss Perrott and Miss Moody, who both passed their exams. So while one missionary's time was used in teaching, others' time was taken up learning language.

Elwood and Bernice had another much needed furlough in the States in 1933. They stayed in Fellowship Homes in Ventnor, New Jersey, just a block from the ocean, a place for furloughing missionaries. They enjoyed the company of others at conferences and social gatherings. Often the talk turned to productive ideas and schemes. Other times everyone was uplifted by wonderful and insightful speakers.

Before heading back to Africa, Elwood and Bernice had the joy of attending some quality spiritual seminars and conferences. Renowned evangelist, radio preacher and camp director Percy Crawford came with his quartet to speak and sing.

Dr. J. Donald Barnhouse—preacher, evangelist and radio speaker—also lectured weekly and the Davises attended his meetings faithfully.

Another joy of furlough was touching base with old classmates. "There is a classmate of mine (living and working) at Cape May. He is a doctor and a Christian. He has a Bible class (with interested neighbors and fellow workers). He has invited us to visit him. Pray as we talk to him that it may be meaningful to us and to the mission work."

During this furlough Dr. Campbell, also an AIM Council Member, performed surgery on Elwood for a double hernia and Elwood writes how his total trust in God gave him great peace of mind. "When I came into the hospital I knew the Lord would be with me and help me and bring me through safely. I had no fear, care or anxiety about the operation or its after effects. I was not at all nervous when I went to the operating room, nor when I began breathing the gas that put me to sleep . . . God has been very good to me and I give Him all the honor and am grateful for the prayers of all who prayed for me."

Even though he was a doctor, a missionary and a leader in church and mission, Elwood was still a warm, emotional man with great love for his sons. On September 30 Elwood writes, no doubt sadly, that, "Perhaps you boys made the wisest decision in not coming up to Ventnor (New Jersey where they were residing) though we did want to see you two very much. There are so many things to talk over and we had so little time together last June."

In October in a letter to Linnell he writes, "It would be so nice to see you, not having seen you for six years and nine months (from age 13 to 20). I have seen so little of you, my first-born son and one who means so much to me and whom I love so much . . ." Elwood and Bernice finally got to see him at Christmas.

From Foot Safaris to Helicopters

Linnell Davis at the first Westervelt home in Indiana in 1926. He was 13 years old and didn't see his parents again until he was 20, six years and nine months later.

Linnell and Philip had chosen to go on a cross country music and promotion tour for the Westervelt Home where they were living. They did meet briefly while touring Pennsylvania.

The Westervelt Boys Band. Linnell is in the centre with the drum and Philip is second from the left with the baritone.

A significant development that helped many missionary parents stay on the mission field was the opening of the Westervelt Home for missionary kids. Mr. and Mrs. Westervelt, who had been dorm parents at Rift Valley Academy in Kijabe Kenya, were forced to stay home due to health concerns. But they did not allow this 'misfortune' to keep them from ministry. Instead, they opened up their home to missionary kids so they could be taken care of by people in whom the mission leadership and parents could be confident, allowing their parents to return to Africa. Some kids found the rules very strict there and did not have a positive time.

But most kids and their parents accepted it as 'good' for the Kingdom. And certainly no parent could say their young person was not well-looked after spiritually and in a disciplined environment. Many future missionary couples came out of the Westervelt Home. My Dad, Linnell, his brother Philip, and my Mom's brother Cedric, all found their spouses at Westervelt. Linnell Davis from AIM in Kenya married Martha Eddings from the Orinoco River Mission in Venezuela. Martha's brother Cedric married Florene McKenrick from AIM in Kenya. And Philip Davis from AIM Kenya married Grace Swanson from the North Africa Mission in Morocco. They all met at the Westervelt Home and gave years of missionary service in Kenya, Venezuela and Brazil, respectively.

When Elwood and Bernice sailed on the *SS Europa* on that wintry day of February 23, 1935, they could not know the serious storm they were to go through. Some of the ship's crew said it was the worst storm in 36 years. Others said the worst in 50 years. One ship received 12 distress calls from other ships in trouble.

But Elwood writes, "We are in Our Father's care and blessing." And then he adds an interesting footnote: "Who knows how many good things came about as a result of the daily prayer meetings of the seven German stewards in the third class baggage room every morning?"

Out at sea and after surviving the storm, Elwood took time to write all the things that they were thankful for. First was "for God leading us down to Brooklyn and the blessings received there and for the speedy and unexpected ways in which our Heavenly Father provided the money for our return to Africa. Not only that, but God provided so abundantly and sufficiently that we are able to travel 'comfortably' (first class). For the $130 extra that was sent to us after our announcement of leaving. For a safe journey across the Atlantic in the worst storm in 50 years." They praised God for a comfortable cabin and for meeting Christians on board. Because staying in a hotel in Southampton, England was so costly, they were thankful they were at sea an extra day and night and so saved that money. They praised God for the many promises they read in His Word in preparation for their next term of service (which ended up lasting over 10 years due to World War II). And last, and not least, was the 60 farewell letters they received."

Finally they arrived at their long-awaited destination of Mombasa. "We docked at 7.45 am (April 4, 1935) and had no trouble with customs as we *knew* the customs official. We received 13 letters from missionaries welcoming us back." One can just sense their excitement at seeing land and feel their hearts throb as the mighty ship sailed almost noiselessly through the narrow channel, providing views of white beaches, palm trees and baobab trees; Fort Jesus and the scents of the African flowers and spices welcoming them home.

"The agent brought us to the Palace Hotel where we had lunch. We saw Dhalla Ismail's son and learned that the family now lives on the mainland. We left by train at 4 pm (for Nairobi). It is nice to be on land again and especially to be in Kenya."

Even with their love for Kenya, for the work, and the fellowship with fellow missionaries and African Christians, getting back also brought the harsh realities of sicknesses, dangers and other problems.

Lee Downing and Elwood Davis in about 1931 at the laying of the cornerstone of the Theodora Hospital with Welles Devitt to the right.

On August 17, 1935, just four months after returning, Elwood records the following sad news: "I am at the end of another week and feeling rather depressed because last night we delivered Mrs. Skoda of a baby girl who was born dead due to complications and a difficult time. This came just two days after Graham Reynolds died of miliary TB (And did I tell you that just last month C. F. Johnstone died of cancer on July 28.) The Reynolds were telegraphed and arrived the next day and the funeral was held at RVA and the local cemetery."

The other reality that came to Elwood was the request to step into the Field Director's position. Mr. Lee Downing, the current director, had lost his wife the previous year and Lee himself was not in good health. Elwood wrote to Linnell asking for prayer and wisdom. "You need to pray much for me. Mr. Downing has been talking about giving up his position as Field Director and that means that others are looking to me to take the job.

"I certainly have my hands so full that I could not take on anything else with my present work. I am not keen on the position and would only want God's will to be done. If He wants me to do that work I will not refuse. The work is so difficult these days that we need special grace to keep up in it."

Elwood stayed in mission leadership for 14 more years, doing medical work, field administration and even running the mission guest house in Nairobi some of the time.

But all was not hardship and heavy responsibility. There were times of progress, fun and harmony with fellow workers. On October 19, 1935 Elwood writes, "All the work is going along fine. School is overcrowded and the church can't hold all the people (now up to 940 members). The hospital is full. The Downing boys (Herbert and Ken) are such a help and blessing. In church I play the organ. Esther Ford, Harry and Daniel Shaffer and Ken Downing play brass instruments. We are praying (and raising money) for a new church."

Adventures are always part of missionary life as well, especially in the old wild days in Africa. When helping at the Maasai station of Siyapei, Bernice writes (tongue in cheek), "It has not been too exciting here at Siyapei." Then she proceeds to tell what **was** happening there. "Last evening as I was walking in front of the house, I heard a lion grunting on the ridge across the river from me. Recently a lion killed a donkey across the river. The day after I arrived, six sheep were killed by a leopard. I have heard hyenas several times. I saw two baboons and have to look out for them daily as they would like to get into the corn. Wild dogs have been heard here these days."

Elwood Davis riding in the back of the car with the Shaffers on safari in Maasai country.

Roy Shaffer and Elwood Davis behind the car on safari.

Despite the adventures with wild animals, thrilling hunting stories, and cultural experiences, by far the most rewarding part of the missionary's life was seeing the changes in the Africans' lives—those to whom they came to minister.

On July 28, 1936, Bernice writes that while they were away from Kijabe at Siyapei the church leaders at Kijabe baptized 20 people and the congregation numbered 1,385 people. And in September she writes that 30 accepted Christ that month, making a total of 280 for the year. "We know it is not by might, nor by power, but by the Holy Spirit of God," she adds.

AIM's missionary conference at Kijabe in 1932. Dr. Elwood Davis is sitting at the back on the left.

In December that year Bernice notes this wonderful news of revival taking place: "In several parts of Africa the Spirit of God is working in a wonderful way. In Rwanda two missionaries and a native worker got together to pray for revival and it started. Now the missionaries are physically worn out taking care of all the new believers. There was so much confession of sin and so many Africans coming to the Lord. They went to the Indian shops and paid their bills and some confessed to stealing (from the shops).

"The Indians came to the meetings because they were so impressed with the African Christians. The two missionaries got permission from their bishop to go to the Divinity School (to hold revival meetings) but the missionary in charge said they didn't need revival as they had 'the cream of the crop of African students.' But revival swept the school, too.

"One of the two missionaries was a doctor and left his medical work to do (fulltime) evangelistic work. There is also a revival in the Baptist work in Congo.

"The European settlers are so impressed with the changes in their African workers that some of the settlers are becoming Christians also."

That revival, often referred to as the East African Revival, swept across much of East and Central Africa and left a lasting legacy of change and church growth for decades to come. There are still some older Africans and missionaries living today who were part of that revival and its results.

While revival was going on in many parts of East Africa in the mid-1930s there were still vast areas where the Gospel had never reached. And there were always more needs to be met; and there were still problems.

Raymond Stauffacher in Congo wrote on July 11, 1936, that, "The field is supposed to be 'occupied by missions' but all we need to do is to tramp out 15 or 20 miles in any direction and you will find in village after village people that have never heard the Gospel before."

Elwood and Bernice Davis (left) Philip (back right) and Linnell (front right).

In Kenya, Bernice writes on July 31, 1936, "Schools are springing up all over the country and especially on the farms. Unless we can put good Christian teachers there, we can't get catechism classes or churches started."

At the AIM Kijabe Conference in March 1936, also during the time of revival, Bernice tells of friction among missionaries. "Well we did have a hard time at conference and following. And there are some things we do not care to talk about except to God. They hurt, especially things that come from fellow missionaries. God can give grace for all these things and we must trust Him for all things."

The year 1936 gave Elwood and Bernice much to look forward to. Linnell would complete university in 1937 and was talking of his plans to return to Kenya as a missionary. He must have mentioned Martha in a letter to his parents because Bernice assured him that whoever he chose, they would love her and receive her as a daughter (after telling Linnell that she hoped he was the one who did the 'picking' and not she!).

Another joy while separated from both their sons was to hear about them from others. Miss Slater, the one in charge of the AIM guesthouse in Nairobi, showed them a letter from friends of hers in Washington, Iowa. Philip was described as being 'so bright and full of cheer' and showing a clear strong personal testimony of his faith in Christ. "How it does our hearts good to hear these good things about our two dear boys at home," Bernice wrote.

A lot of Elwood's time was taken up in traveling far and wide to treat patients. Though he never owned a car, the rail service was excellent and he would also be given rides by others who needed his help.

"After returning to Kijabe (from a hunting trip in the valley) on the 9th of November, I got a telegram from Lumbwa (near Kericho) to go and treat a patient there. I returned the next day, but had a five hour wait in Nakuru and got back to Kijabe at 4 am."

Not all jobs were pleasant, or resulted in healing and had a happy ending. "I was called to the Griswold Williams Estate that Boyce Aggett was managing, to see a white man who was thought to be dead. It turned out he was dead from taking an injection of morphine. Dr. Brown from the Scottish Mission came too and he took care of taking the body to Nairobi."

It was far more enjoyable to help and treat people who recovered and especially ones with whom they had a pleasant relationship. One such was Mr. Wilson, a South African who had run the post office at Machakos and had bought Elwood's mule. Mr. Wilson came to Kijabe for treatments then stayed at Davises during his recovery time.

Other times there was professional cooperation between doctors because of their common interests in medicine and the Gospel. Elwood writes, "Dr. Brown came up to help with an especially delicate operation. He brought a Dr. Mackay with him. Dr. Mackay is the son of Lord Mackay of Scotland of ship building fame. We had the privilege of Dr. MacKay's help on several occasions. He came again in June to help with two abdominal operations."

Even though they had very little income, Elwood and Bernice reminded their son Linnell "to send your tithe money to the Africa Inland Mission to assist missionaries who really need help—like the Sywulkas." Instead of asking for help for themselves, they asked that other needier people be helped.

Bernice also wrote in a November letter, "I am enclosing a dollar bill today for our Christmas present. I hope you will receive from other sources as we are not able to send much."

There was a great spirit of sharing and helping one another. Elwood and Bernice had a cow that gave gallons of milk each day. They gave most of the milk away to others. Others like the McKenricks loved to hunt. Fred was always giving meat away to his fellow missionaries. Some had vegetable gardens from which they shared their produce. The mission also encouraged local workers to have their own gardens and to sell the produce to the missionaries so as to reduce food costs.

"One day Mr. Teasdale and I took a walk to the top of the hill where Maingi does his garden work (this area is now called Maingi town). We were amazed at the view as if from an airplane. Then we walked over to the falls which we had never seen before. These falls are about five miles north from Maingi's gardens."

Adding to the flavor of events, Bernice writes more about family matters and about fascinating people and nature. "Mr. Clarke wanted to send you, Linnell, a Kikamba hymnbook, as you used to sing the hymns when you were younger. Mr. Clarke took over the Mukaa work when we left in 1916 and you were three years old. I thought you might like to sing these songs with the other missionary kids at the missionary meetings. Your brother Philip went on a 15 mile bike ride here at Kaimosi.

"Sir Arthur Conan Doyle (the author of Sherlock Holmes fame) came to Kenya and argued for believing in 'Spiritism' and on 'spiritualism'.

"The locust menace is very big. They have eaten just about everything. Sometimes their group is so large it is six miles wide and 30 miles long."

Truly there was never a dull moment in being a medical missionary in Africa in the early 1900s. While out at Siyapei to help a very sick John Stauffacher, missionaries Lawson Propst and Charles Skoda came by and Mr. Skoda also later came down with a very high fever. Elwood was up all night taking care of the two men. Also while at Siyapei he met a hunter who had been mauled by a lion that had chewed two chunks out of his arm. Finally, a second hunter was able to kill the lion. The wounded hunter took a long time to heal, but went right back to hunting when he had recovered.

Elwood wrote to Linnell and Martha as they traveled in the United States before coming to Kenya requesting that they make a real effort to visit Mr. Moffat in Scranton, Pennsylvania. He was the donor for the Moffat Bible Institute (now Moffat Bible College). This school located in Kijabe continues to train pastors and church workers, sending scores of them into spheres of service for the Kingdom.

Elwood mentioned in 1938 that "Mrs. Watson, who lives at West Pittston and belongs to the new Presbyterian Church there is the woman who gave the money for our hospital (at Kijabe)." Mrs. Watson is the sister to long time AIM US Director Ralph T. Davis.

Supporters like these have always been a real encouragement to missionaries on the field, not only with their financial support, but through their prayers and encouraging letters. Elwood and Bernice had experienced God's faithfulness through their supporters and they wanted Linnell and Martha to have the same encouragement.

Bernice wrote a letter to Linnell on December 1, 1938, from Kijabe.

Dear Linnell,

I don't believe I have written to you for some time, tho' I didn't intend to wait so long but I guess the weeks just <u>rush</u> by.

We were very thrilled at your last letter. It must have been delightful for you to go into Chicago with Dr. Buswell. I couldn't help but think of how cruel you thought I was when I used to make you practice, when you didn't want to. I wonder if I shall ever forget the look on your face at those times! Now your music should be a great comfort and advantage to you, and make you a great blessing too. It can be a snare too, because it is bound to bring you into contact with musical people, and musical people are often emotional and do strange things. We just have to commit you to the Lord day by day, to save you out of all temptations and snares of the evil one. Are you ever going to take any pipe organ lessons, so when you are up against a pipe organ, in your program, you won't be overcome? If you could ever spend any time with Aunt Bertha, she could show you how to manipulate it, at the Dalton church, and with your knowledge of music you could get along.

Don't ever think your work is too routine to write about. You know we are interested in every detail. Is Norman Harrison still there? He was in the glee club and stayed with us when they were in Atlantic City, also a boy whose father was pastor in a church near Reading, where Dr. Becker attends church.

You never say much about Romeyn. Is he enjoying himself as much as you are?

We are having some exciting times around here. I probably wrote you about the woman who was nearly killed by her husband. (It was in my general letter, which got put into *Inland Africa*.) Well, she is staying at the hospital and is doing the cooking for the native girls. Last Sunday a woman stood in church, one of Mwĩiri's nine wives. Another wife was going to stand, but went to the station to buy some clothes 'to stand up' in. When Gathoni (who stood) got home, she got a beating from her husband. Then in a few days the other woman Wanjiku was stripped and strapped to a post and beaten and choked. She came to the hospital and was there a couple of days, then we had a '*cĩra*', a trial, and the sub-chief came. Well, at these trials, there are many words and many lies. Of course, Mwĩiri didn't have a leg to stand on, but there were several old elders there, and the chief didn't want to appear against him too obviously.

Elwood, Mr. Downing, and Mrs. Teasdale were all in Nairobi that day, so Kenneth and I were there besides some of the church elders. Dr. Blakeslee was there for a little while.

The women testified that they were willing to stay at the village and do their work all right, but they insisted on going to church, and refused to do the wicked native customs. Over and over again, the chief or someone else would thunder at them, 'Who bought you? Whose are you?' and they would always answer, 'Mwĩiri,' or 'His,' humbly. Over and over again they said that <u>nothing</u> would ever make them give up the 'things of God.' Andrew and John and Kenneth would get up and speak, and I guess those elders (native) got a lot of gospel they never heard before. The chief was quite a nice young chap and tho' not a Christian is friendly to us. Kenneth got up and spoke and explained to them how the Holy Spirit works in the hearts of people, and how people are willing to suffer for His name's sake, and I couldn't help but think of how Paul stood before Agrippa.

It was wonderful. Well, the chief decided the women better go back to their village, and the *shauri* (matter) was over, but the women said they wouldn't go back unless they would be allowed to come to church. The chief had left to go to the hospital to see a patient and one of the wives started towards the hospital; then I followed and the other wife; Mwĩiri and the maddening crowd went up and they were just seething. Miss Rhodes said she could just <u>feel</u> the power of Satan. Well, I finally told Wanjiku they'd better go home. I knew God could protect them, <u>but</u> I knew also they might be killed. Well, from Friday till Sunday we did a lot of praying. I was sure they would be tied, and not allowed to come. On Saturday old men came to the village and would ask the women if they would give up and they said <u>no</u>. This kept up all day. I guess they thought they would wear them out. Then Mwĩiri told them that they couldn't come to church on Sunday and that if they did there would be a *mutino* (bad luck, accident). So the women ran away in the evening and came to John's village, and came to church in their new clothes. They didn't want to go home, so I have them locked up in the hospital. All over Gikuyuland they are watching the outcome of these three women because there are a lot of women who want to break away and come. They say if the women just hold out against the men, the men can't do a thing but beat them up a bit, and they will get tired of that. Pray much for all the women. The men of course need much prayer; it is the beer drinks they have that hold them back. I forgot to mention that the second wife, Wanjiku, stood up this morning. I'll give you the next chapter next time. We have much to praise the Lord for. We are planning to build a new church. Church now is carried on in three buildings all at the same time. Christmas is over (when you get this) and you are back in school. (I wonder if you went home).

We are soon going to send you the *East African Annual*, a book published every month; when you have read it, send it on to Philip. This number is especially interesting because it shows the picture of the Machakos Fort in the early days, as we knew it. It has been torn down now.

Monday—Another of Mwiiri's wives brought the five little children of the two wives who are here and tried to dump them on to us. He has forbidden any of their children from coming home.

Much love,
From Mother

In all their years in Africa, Elwood and Bernice never experienced any serious illness or accidents. However, when Bernice returned to the US in December 1946 she was diagnosed with cancer. Elwood stayed on in Kenya without Bernice until February 1949 when he went to give personal care to Bernice.

Not many treatments were available in those days, but she managed to live for another three years. Martha Hughell, sister-in-law to longtime US Director Ralph T. Davis, and a nurse, was Bernice's caregiver for several months before leaving to serve in Africa, mostly in Sudan. "Your grandmother was a gracious patient, despite her suffering," Martha told us some 60 years later. Bernice passed away in 1950.

Elwood worked in AIM's home office in Brooklyn, New York, from 1950 to 1954. When Linnell, Martha and we four sons were on furlough in Lancaster in 1954 he had a lengthy stay with us. He then retired to Media, AIM's retirement home in the United States, located just west of Orlando, Florida. He passed away in 1961 in Florida.

The fruit of their ministry is still evident today as we have met some old Maasai from the 1920s and 1930s who were helped by Elwood and Bernice, either at the hospital or on one of their medical safaris. At Longewan in Samburu country we met an old Dorobo woman in her 70s who told us my grandmother had delivered her first child. That child has been the chief at Amaya for the Samburu of that area. Another time we met two old Maasai men on the slopes of Mt. Suswa who told us that Dr. Elwood had treated their families at Kijabe and also visited them down on the plains where they were living.

Looking back, we can see how God used Elwood and Bernice to raise funds in America for the Moffat Bible School at Kijabe as well as the hospital located there—first called the Theodora Hospital, now AIC Kijabe Hospital, a well-known facility throughout all of East Africa. Though they never had much in personal funds they raised the finances necessary for these mission projects.

CHAPTER 4

Challenges of the Forties, Fifties and Sixties

Linnell Davis, my father, headed back to Kenya with his wife Martha in 1938. On Linnell and Martha's first trip to Kenya, Linnell kept a daily journal noting things of interest about their voyage on the *MS Brastagi*. It began in October 1938, with the pastor, Frank C. Torrey, and friends from Calvary Independent Church, Lancaster, Pennsylvania, coming to see them off at the Brooklyn docks in New York City.

1938 prayer card for Linnell and Martha Davis.

Linnell and Martha did not wait until they reached Africa to begin their missionary work. They were traveling with fellow AIM missionaries Rev. Andy Losier, his wife Dorothy, and baby daughter Katherine Anne.

The very first Sunday the Captain gave them permission to lead a church service. Linnell led the service program and Mr. Losier preached, using the Bible story of the shipwreck experienced by the Apostle Paul near the island of Malta, a subject sure to keep one's interest and perhaps to encourage the listener to believe in the God of the Apostle Paul. Andy and his wife Dorothy also sang a beautiful duet and Linnell played a cornet solo. Some of the ship's officers sang a few hymns in their native Dutch language.

"After dinner the Captain invited us to his quarters for a one-and-a-half hour visit. He showed us photos of his home and family and talked about religious conditions in Holland and something of his own attitude. He said when he was a boy he was compelled to attend church and sit through a two hour service. This gave him a distinct distaste for church and spiritual things."

The following Sunday the missionary group again conducted a service in the ship's lounge. Andy Losier led the service while Linnell gave the message. The two women shared their testimonies. There was more special music as well. Linnell wrote, "We are grateful for these opportunities to present the Gospel so that the people on this boat ought not to have any reason or excuse they haven't heard the truth."

The Captain's Dinner, a very fancy affair that took two hours to serve, was provided the evening before arriving in Capetown. The cook and his assistants made beautiful figures out of the food; the ice cream was made into the form of a Dutch windmill. "We hated to spoil it by eating it," was Linnell's comment. During the toasts, one passenger thanked the missionaries for their prayers and for bringing them the Word of God.

After dinner they met in the lounge and sang Gospel songs. The passengers especially enjoyed the duet of Linnell and Martha singing *Resting in His Love*, composed by Blanche Kerr and V. P. Brock.

God has shown His loving face
From His throne in heav'n above
And I've found a resting place
In the shelter of His love.

When the cares of life oppress
When the sky is dark above
I can always find a rest
In the shelter of His love.

O if you were never blest
With this peace from heav'n above
There's for you a wondrous rest
In the shelter of His love.

CHORUS:
I am resting, resting, resting
Sweetly resting in His love
I am resting in His love.

(Special thanks to David and Kathy Ardelean for providing the words of this old hymn).

On Friday, November 11, Linnell arose earlier than usual and was on deck to get his first glimpse of Africa after an absence of 13 years. Later on, when they docked at Durban, Linnell recalled he had been there 18 years previously when he and his parents returned to Kenya. He was seven years old at the time.

Linnell followed in his father's footsteps of keeping track of every detail, and noted the names and a few facts concerning some of the passengers on the *MS Brastagi*. A Mr. Williams from California making his first sea voyage was an author with a great imagination so Linnell felt it was hard to tell whether he was stating fact or fiction! Mr. Williams authored the book **Ambassador of Death**, and gave a copy to Linnell and Martha. Linnell learned later that Mr. Williams' real name was Fishter.

Also on board were Mr. and Mrs. Wiener from New York who were taking a pleasure trip to Java; a young Englishman, 'Rosy', who was trying to grow a moustache and beard in order to appear to look older. He was from Johannesburg and returning from seeing his girlfriend in America. Miss Farmer, an English lady from Johannesburg, and Mr. and Mrs. Piggott, taking a trip to South Africa, were also among the passengers. Mr. Piggott was a retired U.S. Army officer.

On the long ocean voyage Linnell read **Goforth of China**, a biography of Jonathan Goforth who had gone to China as a missionary. Linnell commented, "One cannot help but be stirred by the record of that 'Spirit-filled servant of God.' We realize how small we are and how insignificant. It was obvious in his life that Goforth worked, 'not by might, nor by power, but by My Spirit, says the Lord of Hosts.'" (Zechariah 4:6) This was a tremendous foundational teaching upon which Linnell launched his missionary career.

Linnell and Martha changed ships in Capetown, boarding the *MS Boissevain* and departing Capetown on Thursday, November 17. On this onward voyage to Mombasa they first docked briefly at Port Elizabeth, then East London, followed by a longer stay in Durban, where they purchased pith helmets and visited the botanical gardens. Linnell had visited Durban with his parents in 1920 on their way back to Kenya.

The next port of call was Port Louis in Mauritius. "This island," noted Linnell, "has a curious mix of all kinds of people and nationalities: Africans, Hindus, people wearing turbans and dhotis, Arab traders, Chinese, and European." As it was Sunday, Linnell and Martha and Andy Losier went ashore to look for a church. They worshiped at the Presbyterian Church, though the service was in French.

On Monday, November 28, the ship docked briefly at Réunion Island. They went ashore in the ship's launch to "have a look around and to try and get some stamps." They found the island to be "primitive and dirty" and the service at the post office was less than desirable.

That night as they slept, the ship journeyed on to Tamatave, Madagascar. When they went ashore they "found it just as pretty as it first appeared and entirely different from where we were yesterday. There are many beautiful buildings and the streets are well kept up." At the market they saw many varieties of fruit, as well as souvenirs and products of the island. That afternoon Linnell and the two women enjoyed an hour's ride in a rickshaw.

On the way to Zanzibar, the ship docked briefly to unload cargo at St. Mary, just off the coast of Madagascar. Arriving at Zanzibar on December 3, they found the ship was quickly swamped with all kinds of peddlers selling their wares. Linnell said, "We contented ourselves with just looking at them and listening to the vain pleadings of the salesmen." In the afternoon, the two men went ashore to look around and saw the museum, the old slave market, the bazaars and shops crowded along the narrow streets, the old Portuguese fort, and the Sultan's palace. Linnell enjoyed the chance to speak Swahili and was pleased that he did so well.

December 6th was a BIG day. In his diary Linnell wrote, "This is the day we have been looking forward to for many weeks. We had no alarm clock but guess what happened—we couldn't sleep anyway. At 5.30 Martha and I were on deck as the ship sailed up the narrow channel into Mombasa. There on shore by the Mission Rest Home on the edge of the sea cliff were Mother and Father waving to us. We are really at Mombasa, one of the most beautiful ports in the world."

After unloading and passing through customs they finally met Linnell's parents, Elwood and Bernice. They had lunch and visited and visited. In the afternoon they read the 40 pieces of mail that the steward had handed them as they disembarked. The mail had come to New York after their departure and finally caught up with them.

In the evening they waved goodbye to the *Boissevain* as she sailed by the mission house on her way to the East. Before retiring for the night, the four Davises and the Losiers sang together, read Scripture, and prayed, grateful for their safe arrival. This was Elwood and Bernice's first time to meet Martha. It must have been a thrilling time and a bonding for their future work in Kenya. They had last seen Linnell in the States in 1935, before Martha and Linnell met.

As the Davises and Losiers left Mombasa on the train the following evening, the moon shone brightly. They woke early but it was cloudy and rainy. Reaching Nairobi at 9.30 am they found Welles Devitt and Ken Downing waiting for them. After going to a bank and visiting the American Consul, they had lunch with Miss Slater at the AIM Guest House, leaving for Kijabe as soon as they could! What a moment this must have been for Linnell to share his excitement and joy with Martha, her first time in Kenya! Linnell had been born at Machakos in 1913.

When Linnell and Martha came to Kenya in 1938, just 43 years after the first AIM party arrived in Kenya, they found a large and maturing church from AIM's work as well as from the work of other missions. On January 1, 1939, one of their first Sundays in Kenya, they were at Kijabe and Linnell recorded that in the morning church service, four people stood to profess Christ as Savior. The church at Kijabe was by now 38 years old and the membership was around 1,300.

On Monday January 16, Linnell and Martha attended AIM's week-long annual missionary conference at Kijabe. AIM missionaries were active in medical work, schools, Bible training, evangelism and women's and girls' ministries. There were prayer meetings held every day for the work.

As part of their orientation and while waiting for an assignment to be made, they were encouraged to visit other mission stations and met some prominent people like Chief Njiiri; they also attended meetings with Louis B. Leakey and Canon Beecher.

Chief Njiiri from Kikuyu and his favorite wife in the 1920s.

The most important element in those earlier mission days was the strong emphasis on learning a local language. So on February 17, 1939, at Mukaa, Linnell and Martha began to learn the Kamba language. By this time the mission had opened Bible schools and trained dozens of pastors. On their very first Sunday at Mukaa, a Bible school student did the preaching as part of his training.

Evangelists in Ukambani in the 1940s, with megaphones.

Although language school was very demanding, Linnell spent part of many days hunting birds, bringing back good memories of his childhood around Kijabe.

Language study was interrupted many times, sometimes for visits with the Farnsworths (their language instructors) to outlying schools and churches. Other times they visited Christian elders in the area. But these visits also contributed to language learning because they practiced hearing and speaking Kikamba. Probably the only unwelcome interruption was when Linnell or Martha got sick; Linnell more often, many times suffering from a skin rash that laid him up for days.

Other diversions from language school were hikes to nearby churches, or having visitors come to their station at Mukaa. A couple times Linnell mentions having "a hard time with language." He also talks about the good bonding experience he felt with his language teacher, more especially so because he gave music lessons to the teacher.

Their wonderful conclusion of language school came with the successful completion of five language exams in August, the last one being August 25, 1939.

Linnell and Martha truly began to feel involved and able to contribute to the work when they purchased a vehicle, an old Model T Ford, which they bought for $500 from Mr. Guilding, who was getting ready to go on furlough. This gave them mobility and the opportunity to help others with transportation needs.

September 1939 brought a whole new wave of changes for them, the mission, and indeed the world. War was announced on September 3 and everyone gathered in the evenings around their short wave radios to hear news. Some missionaries were taken into the military because they were either British or Canadian. Others volunteered for military service.

German missionary families were interned—in some cases only the men—while their families were left under house arrest. Gerald May, an age mate of ours from Rift Valley Academy, lost his Dad to the intern camps in Southern Rhodesia for four long years. "Every German was assumed to be a spy," Gerry told me.

The Next Generation of Davis Men Are Born in Kenya

During the time Linnell was teaching at the Machakos Bible School, from 1939 to 1942, their first-born son, Van, was born on May 16, 1940. Mother went to Kijabe for the birth to have the professional care and personal touch from her parents-in-law, Dr. Elwood and Nurse Bernice.

A year and a half later, I (Arthur) was born at Machakos on November 14, 1941; Bernice traveled there to act as midwife.

Both Van and I had real trouble digesting any kind of milk and we were near death a couple of times. Finally a milk made from formula helped Mother to keep us alive.

When Raymond, the third son, was born on October 12, 1945, Linnell took Martha to Nairobi for the delivery. On July 13, 1951 Allan, the fourth son was born, also in Nairobi.

Boyhood Memories

When Linnell took us sons along on his school supervision safaris, we would usually go out hiking or hunting in the area around his meeting place. On Sundays we would leave the service early to get a bite to eat at the outdoor cooking area where the feast was being prepared.

Church members at the Peter Cameron Scott Memorial Chapel at Nzaui in the 1950s.

I have vague memories of my first voyage to America in 1946, when I was five years old. We traveled on an American freighter carrying only 12 passengers. In 1946 it was still believed there were

German U-boats in the Atlantic. So every few days, we would have a boat drill. I remember being really scared and crying a lot.

Families who traveled during those years always divided up in case there would be a catastrophe at sea. So, leaving Kenya in September 1946, my older brother Van and I traveled with Dad. Mother had gone in July with Ray, the youngest son at the time.

On our return to Kenya in 1948, Ray and I went with Mother while Van traveled with Dad. I remember finding an expensive (according to my Mom) gold watch and hoping to keep it. But Mother insisted it should be returned to its rightful owner, a valuable lesson for me to learn early in life. So she took it to the Captain who promised to go through the ship's passenger list looking for a name with the initials 'M.L.' that were engraved on the back of the watch. To my extreme delight no one was located to claim the watch and the Captain allowed me to keep it! I held onto it for a long time, hoping to make a fortune from it, but somewhere in our many moves it got misplaced.

I have vivid memories of a near death experience when I was 10 years old and suffering from a combination of typhoid, amoebic dysentery and malaria. The rest of the family had gone to visit another missionary living on the same station at Mukaa and I was alone.

I must have been delirious and I dreamed I was in my double-decker bed turned on its end, leaving me clinging to the bedsprings above me. At the bottom of the bed was a very deep hole, and at the bottom of the hole was a man from China dressed in a long robe and wearing a pigtail and mustache. He told me if I let go and dropped into the hole, I would die and be in Hell forever. I really clung to those springs with all my strength! I must have fallen into a deeper sleep. Next thing I remember was Mother waking me. I was glad to be alive. As I told her my dream, she lovingly reassured me I could never lose my salvation and Satan used such nightmares to frighten me.

In December 1950 my brother Ray and I shared an event that was to have eternal significance. Our family went on vacation to Mombasa every December for two weeks, usually with one or two other missionary families. This year, the Sheldon Folk and Carroll

Ness families joined us in the old mission 'Fort,' a two story building with several large bedrooms, right near Likoni Channel, the route of all ships entering and leaving the port of Mombasa.

Ray and I had gone snorkeling and spear fishing from Shelly Beach. We had enjoyed the most successful catch of our young fishing careers. We carried a couple dozen surgeon fish, parrot fish and zebra fish in our *kikapu* (woven basket). We also had some colorful leopard and helmet shells, scorpion shells and a variety of other shells.

As the tide came in and the water was up to our knees on the outer reef, we decided to head in. But instead of returning to shore using the route we had taken out to the reef, we took a shortcut. (Time for an African truism—shortcuts are never shorter.)

As we headed back to shore, we kept falling into deeper and deeper pools of water. Sometimes they would be over our heads, but each time we quickly came out the other side of the deep pools.

When we were about three-fourths of the way in, we went into a deep pool and had to start swimming. Ray didn't know how to swim well. I had the *kikapu* full of fish and shells and also carried the spear gun. The urge to survive quickly identifies priorities! First, I dropped the *kikapu*, and a few meters later the spear gun. But there was still no end to this one pool (years later we learned this deep channel is nearly half a mile long and a quarter mile wide).

Ray and I could see the shore. We saw fishermen mending their nets. We cried and yelled, but they didn't move to help us. "Crazy *wazungu* playing while we have to work our heads off," they may have thought.

Just when it seemed we were finished, our strength gone, and drowning our fate, we saw a white man dressed in white clothes standing by the fishermen talking to them. In an instant these men jumped up and came to their canoe at the water's edge, pushed it into the water, and headed towards us!

That scene kept us from giving up. Oddly enough, just as they reached us, we reached the other side of the channel and stood up, waist high in water.

Ray told us later that during our struggle against drowning he cried out to Jesus to forgive his sins and save his soul. The evidence of his life since that moment has proved the genuineness of his profession of faith. The man in white had gone by the time we reached the shore and we've often wondered if he wasn't an angel.

When my parents worked in Kamba country, they ran into a lot of witchcraft, mostly practiced by women. As in most cultures, there are good and bad diviners, alleged healers, and others who can curse you so you die. My Aunt Florene's Dad, Fred McKenrick, was cursed by a Kamba witchdoctor. But she also 'enforced' her curse by giving him poison through another person. He nearly died, but recovered and had many more years of fruitful ministry in Kenya.

Elwood had retired from the field and Bernice had passed away in 1950 when the ugly head of traditional practices rose again in Kenya in October 1952 in the guise of nationalism. This movement was called the Mau Mau. Members of this group got their power and impetus from hideous oathing ceremonies that included drinking of human blood, cutting themselves, and binding themselves as blood brothers swearing to kill Christians, whites and government officials and all people loyal to the British government.

In the course of this five-year uprising over 55,000 Kikuyu people were slaughtered including government police; dozens of European and British soldiers were brutally killed, sometimes by dismemberment while still alive, severing limbs and private parts, we were told by police. European settlers and farmers who died numbered somewhere under 100.

I was a teenager living in Kikuyu country during this time and saw things first hand and heard stories of these hideous Mau Mau practices. It was a frightening time in our lives.

The boarding school (RVA) even sent us home one term because there were so many threats. Many mission leaders, including my Dad (Linnell) and his colleagues received threatening letters from the Mau Mau, even telling them they were targeted to be killed.

However, instead of scaring off missionaries and causing church leaders to leave, these threats had the opposite effect. Missionaries stayed in Kenya and new members joined the mission during these days. The African church leaders stood firm, even in the face of persecution and many gave their lives, rather than give up their faith in Jesus Christ. They really did believe Christ's claim of being the Savior of the world and that His death and resurrection were real events and it all *'was really true.'*

No doubt the firm foundation laid by those early missionaries—Elwood and Bernice Davis, Mr. Waechter, the Shaffers, Hurlburts, Downings, Teasdales, Skodas, Stauffachers, Andersens, Barnetts, Propsts, among others—did bear fruit and the African church grew both in numbers and in spiritual depth.

Most Christians survived the attacks and persecutions of the Mau Mau; others gave their lives because they refused to renounce Jesus Christ and take the oath required by the Mau Mau, who traveled in large armed groups. Empowered by the oaths they took and often stimulated by drugs, they traveled in bands to villages of their own people demanding that they join their group or be killed. Thousands were killed every month at the height of their atrocities.

During the height of the Mau Mau, in 1953, when the worst atrocities were taking place, a large group planned to kill the whites living at Kijabe, including the 90 or so missionary kids. On that fateful night, over 1,000 Mau Mau attacked a large settlement of their own people at Lari, five miles from Kijabe. They had a dual plan: to wipe out those Kikuyu living at Lari who were loyal to the colonial government, and then to kill the whites living at Kijabe Mission Station.

They broke through the weak protective fencing at Lari and in a night of carnage and mayhem killed 212 of their own, most of them women and children, cut many into pieces, disemboweled pregnant women and dashed children's heads against rocks.

I was 12 years old at the time and was present in the school that night. We kids were awakened from sleep sometime after midnight and told to meet downstairs by the fireplace in the old large double story dorm and classroom building known as Kiambogo (place of the buffalo). Teddy Roosevelt, US president from 1901-1909, had laid the cornerstone of the building 44 years earlier, in 1909. One older boy, Don Hoover, was given a .22 caliber rifle and visiting missionary Charlie Hess had another to protect us. As we woke, we were told only that a large gang of Mau Mau was coming and we should gather to pray. The government had put a small contingent of Kenyan police on the station with a British officer in charge. Several months earlier they had also asked the mission to surround the school with a barbed wire fence.

All of us younger boys were guarded in the lower north room of the bottom of Kiambogo building. Some of the older boys patrolled outside with guns. We smaller boys all had our slingshots with marbles, confident that we could beat any number of Mau Mau who might break through the outer defenses of the school compound. Little did we know how serious our situation was! Nor did we know on that night what an amazing thing God was doing to protect us.

We had no knowledge of the fact that this group of fearless Mau Mau had already broken through the barbed wire fence and other village defenses at Lari and overcome the police force there. And we had no idea there was such a large number of Mau Mau running toward us, many of them carrying guns. After nearly two hours waiting by the unlit fireplace, we were told we could go back to bed because the Mau Mau had fled after reaching the perimeter of the station.

In the days following, we learned an amazing story of how the Mau Mau was indeed turned away. As they swooped down on the station, the first group met an astonishing sight. A wall of hundreds of men, dressed in bright white robes and holding spears with flaming tips totally blocked their path. Afraid and realizing they could not penetrate that wall of warriors, the Mau Mau scattered, many dropping their weapons, and fled in all directions. It appears our school had been protected by an army of angels!

Two men were captured by police as they were fleeing from the edge of the station. These captured Mau Mau each told this story to the police and repeated it to some of the missionary men later. Welles Devitt, an AIM missionary from Kijabe, related the full story to us and Billy Graham included this amazing story in his book, **Angels**.

Over the next few months as AIM missionaries ministered to captured Mau Mau prisoners in the prison camps, they heard the same story several times. In a Sunday service at RVA, AIM missionary Jim Bisset told us of hearing this story when meeting a prisoner in a camp. Another confirmation was given to me at the Driftwood Club in Malindi by the late Jean Davies, whose husband Peter, a fluent Kikuyu speaker, had interrogated prisoners. "The story of the Mau Mau seeing angels at Kijabe is absolutely true," she said. "My husband heard it firsthand from several of the prisoners."

The buildings of Rift Valley Academy were surrounded by a wire fence 10 feet high. Just past the high fence was a moat five feet deep and five feet wide, filled with pointed bamboo stakes. Outside of that was a three-foot-high roll of barbed wire. There were four sand-bagged police lookouts at the corners that were manned 24 hours. We had 24 Kenyan police and one British inspector in charge.

We felt well protected, but stories of continuing atrocities kept our fears and adrenalin at a high level.

The policemen lived below the Kiambogo building, just under the dining room, which also served as a study hall at night. One evening at about 8 pm, while we were diligently doing our homework, a gun went off from below us and a bullet came up through the floorboards and passed between two students sitting at the dining tables.

The British inspector who was with us in the study hall jumped up instantly and using a few choice words of 'the King's English' descended to the barracks demanding an explanation. The African policeman had the ultimate answer. "Bwana," he blurted out, "the devil got into my gun."

"He sure did," yelled the inspector, "and now you better give me that gun before another devil gets into it."

One time we went on patrol with this same policeman, Anthony (Tony) Vernon Wood Pepper, a colorful law officer in His Majesty's colonial government who took his job very seriously. He had joined the Kenya police force by lying about his age (an officer had to be 21 years old; Tony was only 19). He wore a moustache which made him look older. But he was a good officer and well-qualified for his job.

One day during the August holiday in 1955, he invited Howard Andersen, a friend and seventh grade classmate of mine, and me to go on patrol with him. Our parents lived on Kijabe Mission Station, so we were there during the school holiday. We headed off below the mission station to the old railway cut, each carrying a gun. When we reached the old railway line, Tony took his .303 British Enfield rifle and started to shoot through the old tunnels that had been built over small *dongas* (elongated ditches).

"This will scare the Mau Mau and make them think we've killed some of their number," he said. "Also, I learned in demolition school that the shot from a high powered rifle can collapse a tunnel like this." Nothing collapsed, however, and after a couple tunnel shootings, using all his .303 shells, he handed the gun to Howard and then pulled out his pistol. Spread throughout the African plains is a small green bush that bears many yellow marble-sized balls. Tony started picking some of them off with accurate shots from his pistol. Soon he was out of cartridges for the pistol. But he still had the 'greener gun' (a shotgun with very large shot for stopping people or animals). Tony again and with great skill began to pick off doves, mousebirds and turacos with his shotgun. When he had one shell left he turned to Howard and me saying, "We better save this in case we meet any Mau Mau." Howard and I stared wide-eyed at each other because we still had over 75% of the patrol ahead of us!

But with that cocky assurance of the mighty British Empire behind him, Tony set off, striding confidently, with us walking meekly and scared in single file behind him. Thankfully we survived that patrol.

Perhaps the closest I felt I came to being killed by the Mau Mau occurred when I was only 11 years old and a month before the 'emergency' was declared in Kenya on October 20, 1952.

John Barnett, Jackie Losier and I were purchasing candies at the old railway station *duka* (a small shop) three miles from the school. And we had gone off the school grounds without permission, as we often did. Perhaps we shared in the universal feeling that wrongdoing is only a problem if you get caught.

Well, we were young sinners at the time and we bolted out of the *duka*, dodging behind the building to avoid being seen by 'Pa Herb' (Herbert Downing, the principal of the school) who quite unexpectedly drove up. But now we had to take a bush path back to school to avoid being caught by him as he returned to school on the road. As we made our way along the bush path, we talked about how we may have been seen by Pa Herb and that fearful punishment would be awaiting us when we reached school.

Suddenly we met five Kikuyu men, all armed. Three carried *pangas* or *simis,* (long sharp knives) and two had guns that looked like .303 military rifles. "We are going to kill you!" one of them shouted. All of us were born and grew up in Kenya and up to this point in our lives none of us had known anything but friendly and respectful Africans. So we didn't really think he was serious. But as they came toward us with menacing looks and hate in their eyes, Jackie Losier quietly said, "There's a turn in the path here, let's run for it."

And run we did! Too bad the Olympic scouts were not timing us, because we would have broken all records. We ran for over a mile as fast as we could without looking back.

When we finally came to a panting halt, we were really scared. We ran more slowly all the way back to the school and by now had forgotten any fear of 'Pa Herb'. This all happened the first week of September 1952, just a month before the Mau Mau movement was officially declared to be illegal and Jomo Kenyatta, its purported leader, was jailed.

During the years of the Mau Mau rebellion, my parents went on furlough to the US in February, 1954, and we passed through the Suez Canal. I was 12 years old at the time and I remember swimming in the pool and playing deck games. When we crossed the equator, one of the sailors dressed as King Neptune and presided over a party. The *Gully Gully* man came aboard at Port Sudan in the Red Sea and entertained us with all kinds of tricks. Being a first class magician, he certainly fooled us kids. Divers in the waters along the

From Foot Safaris to Helicopters

Sudanese ports dove for money and trinkets thrown to them by the passengers.

When we reached England, Mr. Wilson, one of the wealthy passengers, invited our family to see television—the very first time we had ever seen such an amazing thing. We sat and happily watched a boxing match on a black and white television set.

On our return trip to Africa in 1955, I was 13 years old and enjoyed the journey even more. Charles Lamb, a well-known author, was one of the passengers. But we were not aware of how important he was and we were still too young to appreciate all his wisdom. He very kindly condescended to talk to us, regaling us with great stories.

I also remember passing through several serious storms. As a young teen with limited knowledge and even less trust in the strength of man's creations versus God's storms, I was not sure we would survive! The first one occurred our first night out of New York aboard the mighty *Queen Elizabeth II*. The second happened on board the *Braemar Castle* as we traveled through the Bay of Biscay. And the third storm hit as we were docked at Genoa in Italy. There the Captain decided it would be better to leave harbor before the storm hit, and that turned out to be a good decision. Several large ships were damaged in port and a few were overturned in the water. We got far enough away that we were not too badly affected by that storm.

We had a spectacular view of Mount Vesuvius on the western coast of Italy. This active volcano has erupted more than 50 times since its first outburst in AD 79.

When I was 17, I nearly went the way of many a hunter in the African bush at the end of a rhino horn. We were hunting in Block 32 with missionary Henry Hildebrandt. My brother, Ray, was along as well as his friend, Jon Machamer. On this particular day, Jon and I hunted together while Ray went with Henry.

Jon and I were tiptoeing gingerly along a rough path, peering ahead for the much-prized lesser kudu antelope. The bush was dense and green. Suddenly from close behind us and to our left the bushes erupted noisily and out of the corner of my eye I saw a rhino headed straight for me! I bolted forward on the path, expecting to be airborne on the rhino's horn any instant. I tripped on a tree root and fell headlong onto the path, my gun plowing into the dirt barrel first ahead of me.

Why I wasn't trampled by the startled rhino I'll never know, apart from God's protecting me. But perhaps when I fell, I disappeared from his sight, because the rhino just kept on going on a parallel path to my left. Jon had gone further to my right. We were badly shaken but glad to be alive. In our youthful confidence, we just continued to hunt.

Around this time we were at Kijabe after RVA closed because the annual missionary conference was to be held there. All missionaries, including our parents, would attend. We kids had a couple sessions, but mostly went on hikes, played games, or sat around telling stories. One day one of my best friends, Paul Barnett (son of Erik Barnett) asked several of us if we wanted to go with him to the old station to get candies and drink *chai*, the widely-popular East African drink of tea, milk and sugar. We quickly agreed to that idea! Paul had recently learned to drive. We had driven with him several times and knew him to be a careful driver.

On the way back, we came to a place called second ravine and the car came close to the ravine's edge. There was a soft shoulder and before we knew it, we were plummeting down this 500-foot steep incline. But it seemed as if God slowed down the car and guided it into a tree that caught the side of the car and brought it to a stop. Paul had not been driving fast. Miraculously—even without the use of modern seatbelts—no one was hurt. Our biggest fear was telling Paul's Dad what had happened. We walked slowly back to the station all agreeing to defend our driver. Paul's Dad, I think, was so relieved that no one was hurt or injured that he reacted quite calmly and asked Doc Propst (Dr. Jim Propst, a medical doctor and station maintenance man) to tow the vehicle back to the station with his big 4X4 army truck dubbed 'The Rhino.'

From Foot Safaris to Helicopters

Linnell and Martha

My parents' greatest joy and fulfillment came from the hundreds of Africans who were trained to be pastors and taught the 'whole doctrine of God.' They first taught students in several Bible schools throughout the Kamba area. In 1962 Dad was given the task of starting Scott Theological College, now the premier Bible University of the Africa Inland Church in Kenya. Linnell served for several years as the first principal of Scott College; later, he went back to teach for several additional years. Mother taught at Ukamba Bible School.

AIM's interfield conference in about 1958 in Kampala. Linnell Davis is in centre.

After some 30 years in Kamba country, in the late 1960s Linnell was asked to move into an administrative role in the mission. They lived in Nairobi where he was the Field Director for Africa Inland Mission.

The trophies he and Mother received for their 38 years of work in Kenya are truly known only to God; others of their converts and students are busy doing the work of pastors, evangelists and teachers, because of my parents' dedication and commitment. From my earliest memories, I can see Dad traveling to meetings, sitting for long hours and traveling home again. Even at home, he had a continuous train of people coming to see him, to ask for advice or for his words to be spoken in a council meeting.

But perhaps his most rewarding time was his last four years in Kenya as he traveled all over Kamba country teaching Bible to church leaders in TEE (Theological Education by Extension) classes; TEE was an in-service type of training. The men came together once a month for several days, were able to share their experiences, prayer requests and vision with each other, get Bible training, and return to their churches to put the new ideas and teaching into practice.

One of the first graduating classes from Scott Theological College in the 1960s.

I had graduated from RVA in 1960 and from Lancaster Bible College in 1964. After two years at Elizabethtown College, I was studying religious journalism at Syracuse University. In 1968 I was asked by Dr. Bob Laubach of Laubach Literacy to join the group traveling to Kenya for an *AfroLit* Conference. My first trip 'home' since 1960! I was super excited and eager to go.

At the conclusion of the *AfroLit* Conference I accompanied my Dad as he traveled to different centers to teach Bible classes to pastors and evangelists. I attended two of Dad's TEE classes, one in Kitui near Mwingi and the other at Kikambulyu. In both instances I could see Dad really enjoyed teaching and interacting with the students. I could also see they were very keen and attentive. They not only loved the teaching; they loved their teacher.

Linnell Davis and his TEE class in 1968 in Kibwezi area.

Daniel was one of the pastors who had come out of his traditional culture with its life of fear, worship and praise of ancestors as promoted by witchdoctors. He had heard about Jesus Christ from my parents, who had told him that Jesus is God's Son, had lived on earth, was killed by the cultural and religious leaders of his day, and rose again after three days to prove He is God and therefore could redeem mankind.

Pastor Daniel took Dad and me to meet an older woman witchdoctor who just the previous day had believed in Jesus Christ as her Savior. She requested Pastor Daniel to oversee the burning of all the charms, amulets and other artifacts she used in her practice of witchcraft in front of us, the local pastor and all her neighbors. Dad translated the testimony she shared as her whole life's beliefs, practices and source of income went up in flames.

Another woman we visited was the mother of a Bible School student, a very bright young man who went on to study under my Dad at Scott Theological College in Machakos. Later he became a prominent church member and the chaplain to former president Daniel arap Moi. This woman, his mother, was one of the 'blessing' diviners, considered a friend of the people. She showed us her 'bag of tricks' which was a gourd filled with river pebbles, smooth stones of different colors. She demonstrated how she had used them to practice her trade. She rattled the stones in the gourd, and then threw them on the ground. The way they landed—which colors went where and all that—revealed a prophecy. She would predict when rains would come, someone would find his lost goat and what medicine to give to a sick relative. This was all very interesting but offered little insight beyond common sense.

At the Kikambulyu TEE classes near Kibwezi an elder's gardens were being destroyed by wild pigs. The men agreed to pray about it and the next time they met, the elder reported that no wild pigs had come at all in the past month.

Linnell had a tremendous advantage in teaching Bible to the Kamba elders. He understood and used fluent Kikamba. He had helped translate the Bible into Kikamba as well as the Kikamba hymnbook. He was never bored as he moved to new places every few days. The stories were always new and different at each teaching location. The students came from varying backgrounds, lived in different areas and brought fresh stories, ideas and vision.

A reading of Linnell's diaries of all his travels during this time could wear you out! He had to have *loved* traveling. Mother enjoyed staying at home teaching the women, being active in the Cadettes program for the girls, and hosting her many missionary and African friends who frequently came by.

The thing that made all the travel possible was that petrol (gasoline) was only six shillings per gallon and the fact that he used his faithful Volkswagen, which gave him 40 miles to a gallon.

Linnell was a slow and methodical driver and rarely went over 50 mph. This, too, gave him better gas mileage. As kids we remember it seemed to take forever to get home or to any destination with Dad driving! But we also never felt afraid or even thought of the possibility of an accident.

Although he spent several years in mission leadership, acting as Field Director on two occasions, Linnell's heart was with the Africans and especially the church people. He never seemed to tire of endless meetings with church, school and government leaders. As we have had our own career in missions and seen that of many others, we still are amazed at how our folks endeared themselves to the people without giving them any money, school fees or sponsoring projects. They simply just did not have any money to give! But they gave their time, probably the most precious thing a person can give in Africa. When they would visit their former students in their places or ministry, they had only godly counsel and Biblical advice to hand out, and actually it would be the pastors and churches who would bless them with gifts of papaya, maize, guavas, honey or chickens. As kids we saw this happen frequently.

From 1948 to 1962 Linnell traveled all over Machakos district, supervising schools, attending school board meetings and insuring there were Christian headmasters in all the 103 schools he oversaw. He traveled in old pickup trucks and later in the newest German car on the market, the Volkswagen. Mrs. Evelyn Davis (the wife of Bill Davis) did the same for all of Kitui District. They were given petrol money by the government.

When he visited schools, Linnell took the opportunity to also meet with church leaders and encourage them. He often attended their council meetings and was frequently asked to speak in their churches and the men's conferences.

Martha and other missionary women organized massive women's conferences, often attended by over 5,000 women. There were very few buses in those days, but these women came from all over Ukambani to receive sound biblical teaching from the missionary women and godly older Kamba women.

I distinctly remember one conference at Mumbuni where over 5,000 women attended. They decorated the ground with their colorful dresses just as the purple petals of the jacaranda tree do in October.

Women's conference at Machakos in 1956.

After completing 38 years of missionary work in Kenya, Linnell and Martha returned to the States in 1976 to care for Martha's 86-year-old mother Gara Eddings, herself a retired missionary from Venezuela, where Martha was born. Her husband, Van, had passed away in California in 1972. Linnell and Martha thought they would soon be able to return to their work in Kenya. But thanks to their loving care, Gara lived to be 100 years and passed away in 1992. The Davises never returned to fulltime missionary work in Kenya.

Sweeping spectacular scenery is enjoyed for a time. The beauty of a lion on the plains is soon forgotten. The thrill of a trophy kill is passing. The stories of great experiences of the past get old and are outdone by other experiences. But the redemption of one human soul is for eternity and the Bible says the angels in Heaven rejoice over the news of one new person believing in Jesus.

That is why four generations of Davis related families have lived in Africa and South America for nearly 100 years—for the high calling of telling people the good news of eternal life through faith in Jesus Christ. And this is why two generations are still working in Africa and the next generation is being prepared to carry on the work into the end of the 21st century.

Linell and Martha with Allan, Art, Ray, Van (left to right). 1997

Chapter 5

The Third Generation Takes Over

In all our years growing up in Kenya money was never plentiful, yet we never lacked for clothes, school fees or food. While we all had the African ailments like malaria, dysentery and fevers, we were never without adequate treatment and care.

All four Davis sons attended the Rift Valley Academy (RVA) at Kijabe, Kenya, where Elwood and Bernice had worked in the hospital for so long. Van and I started at RVA in January 1948; Ray joined us in 1952 and Allan in 1957.

We were well known for our sports abilities at RVA, but it was the youngest, Allan, who outshone us all with his goals scored in soccer, tries in rugby and baskets in basketball. Allan didn't enjoy the academic part of RVA, but Assistant Principal Hal Cook made his life at RVA enjoyable. Some staff wanted to bar students below a certain grade point average from playing sports. Hal felt that if Allan were kept from his sports he would not do as well in academics. By being permitted to continue with the sports program Allan improved his grades in classes and played his heart out on the ball field.

After graduation from high school at RVA and various colleges in the US, Van, Ray and Art all returned to the mission field in Kenya with the Africa Inland Mission. Allan served in the US Army and now lives with his family in Alabama, and has become a first class aviation mechanic.

My older brother Van with his wife Kathy served at Machakos briefly before moving to Mulango where there were nine single lady missionaries who taught in the government school and the Bible school. Besides being actively involved in church ministry, Van was the station handyman.

From there they moved to Mombasa for a short time before being assigned to Malindi where they have served for over 35 years. At Malindi Van was asked to be the treasurer of the local church and later for the district. Van's heart for reaching the unreached was evident in the starting of fellowships in the interior and later building churches for them. Van was always the mechanic for visiting missionaries and the handyman to the Europeans living in Malindi. He also conducted services Sunday evenings for the European community.

Ray returned to Kenya in 1970 and was assigned to the Turkana District. When he and Jill were married in 1973 they continued working in Turkana at Kalokol until 1982. They learned the Turkana language, helped start new churches in the 'bush' and led Bible studies and leadership training for the Turkana Christians.

The Davis clan at Lake Naivasha for a reunion in 1986. Back row: Linnell and Ted. Second row from back: Art, Ray, Van. Third row from back: Mary Ellen, Jill, Martha, Kathy. Fourth row from back: Caroline, Kristin, Karen. Front row: Christy, Patty-Leigh, Daniel, Jeff

In 1982 they moved to Amaya, where my wife Mary Ellen and I had started a ministry among the Pokot people. We had been asked to move to Nairobi where I served as the Africa Inland Church Missionary Board (AICMB) Coordinator. Ray and Jill's years in Pokot were productive as they trained leaders and young people in the growing Pokot church. Together we launched the Churo High School, with the donations of Paul and July Land from Holland, Michigan.

Ray and Jill now teach at the Africa Inland Church Missionary College in Eldoret, training pastors and their wives to serve effectively as missionaries in other cultures.

Art and Mary Ellen and the Pokot

The lives of all my brothers and their families could fill books of their own. But I will focus on how God led me back to Africa and our work among the Pokot people.

Every teenage white boy in Kenya during the 1930s to the 1960s idolized the renowned professional hunters and wanted to be one of them. My hero was J.A. Hunter, who lived near Makindu. I met him on only one occasion, in 1960, when missionary George Machamer and I were hunting near Kiboko, which means hippo in Swahili. We came upon J.A. Hunter with some guests. He was excitedly showing his visitors a two-foot long tortoise, explaining its characteristics and habitat in great detail.

One of the most renowned of all African hunters, J.A. Hunter had killed over 800 rhinos (many at the government's request), 500 lions, over 1500 elephant and a couple thousand buffalo. Now he was a kinder, gentler, white-haired gentleman in his 80s, retired at his home near Kiboko.

J.A. had led hunting safaris for princes, dukes and duchesses, film stars, millionaires, renowned English lords and American politicians. He had endured extreme hardships, many close calls and saved many clients' lives. He was a hero to many.

In contrast to J.A. were missionaries like George Machamer, my parents and grandparents and their colleagues. They had no great hunting stories, no famous clients, and not much in earthly possessions. But today when we visit the hunting areas of J.A. Hunter, not many have heard of him. In contrast, many HAVE heard of the Machamers; the churches they built and the leaders they led to faith in Christ are all throughout that area.

George and Dot Machamer learned the Kamba language and spoke it fluently. They held preaching services in the markets. They visited hundreds of homes and villages. In 30 years they saw many Kamba people come to know Christ. The Machamers trained many leaders, who then trained others. Dozens more churches have been built by their students in the faith and by their students' students. While J.A. had many great animal trophies, the Machamers had hundreds more 'people' trophies, some who are now in Heaven while others are still active in ministry. While J.A. had many great stories written about him, and he himself authored several books, the Machamers' stories are recorded in Heaven. While J.A. hosted great leaders, widely known and famous personalities, the Machamers led the unknown, humble and ordinary Kamba person to greatness in the Kingdom of God.

I longed to be like J.A. Hunter, but God blocked that path and led me instead in the footsteps of my grandparents, parents and missionaries like the Machamers. My Aunt Florene (McKenrick) Eddings' father, Fred McKenrick, came to Kenya in 1905. He was also a hunter, but did it to supply meat for the missionaries and the needier Kenyan people. Together with his hunting skills he also preached and taught the Bible, baptizing hundreds of Kenyans. Fred also oversaw the building of churches, classrooms and dispensaries.

When Elwood Davis retired at 70 years of age, his sons continued the missionary tasks their father had inspired in them. Linnell served in Kenya for 38 years, while Philip went to Brazil as a missionary for over 30 years.

Van Eddings' daughter, Martha, married Linnell and worked with him in Kenya, while his son Cedric married Fred McKenrick's daughter Florene and they worked in Venezuela for over 30 years.

Cedric Eddings on his ham radio at the headwaters of the Orinoco River in Venezuela where they worked as missionaries for many years.

Florene Eddings on the three-week boat trip to their mission station at the headwaters of the Orinoco River in Venezuela.

When I graduated from RVA in July 1960 I wanted to stay in Kenya and become a professional hunter and lead famous people on hunts in my beloved Kenyan hunting paradise, like my hero J.A.

Hunter. Since my parents would not hear of that, I traveled with them to the US in 1960 when they went on their furlough.

The trip included a flight to Egypt to see the pyramids, the Sphinx and other old world wonders. We also went to Jordan to tour the Holy Land. We stayed at Mrs. Lambie's Guest House in Bethlehem; the Lambies had served in the Holy Land their entire adult lives and now Mrs. Lambie, a widow, was carrying on the work alone and running the guesthouse as well.

I entered Lancaster School of the Bible in Lancaster, Pennsylvania, in September 1960 and worked my way through those four years of college. During those four years, I was marvelously persuaded by my pastor, Frank C. Torrey, godly teachers at Lancaster Bible College, and Africa Inland Mission leaders Rev. Sid Langford, Rev. John Gration, and A.B. Holm to follow in the footsteps of my parents and grandparents. I remain thankful to God and his people for helping me to make right choices.

While in Bible College, I met Mary Ellen Huber, my future wife. We were married June 11, 1965, and we both shared the strong conviction of going to the mission field. I was encouraged by Dr. Bob Laubach to first study journalism at Syracuse University. This invitation came when I attended an Evangelical Literature Overseas (ELO) conference in Marion, Indiana.

While I studied at Syracuse, having financial aid with an assistantship from the Laubach Literacy Foundation, Mary Ellen taught in an elementary school in nearby Onondaga.

After graduation from Syracuse, I worked as a reporter for two years with the *Syracuse Herald Journal*, followed by one year with the *Lancaster Intelligencer Journal* (Lancaster, PA)—all to get experience in writing in preparation for future work on the mission field. During these years, our daughter Kristin was born in Syracuse, New York, on December 6, 1969, and our daughter Karen was born in Lancaster, Pennsylvania, on January 23, 1971, both on cold and snowy nights!

Rev. John Gration of the Africa Inland Mission then asked us to attend a missionary internship training program in Farmington, Michigan, in order to improve our cultural and inter-personal skills.

This nine-month program was the single best preparation I had for the mission field and we have been forever grateful to the AIM for requiring us to go there.

We traveled to Kenya in August 1972 and attended Swahili language school from September to December at the Anglican Church of Kenya Language School in Nairobi. From there we were assigned to the mission literature department at Kijabe. I worked as a writer for *Today in Africa* and *Afrika ya Kesho* magazines. The editor at the time was Ed Arensen; Phil Lasse was a renowned artist; fellow writers were Hal Olsen and John Ndeti; Jack Wilson was a new artist. It was a stimulating and adventurous time as I traveled all over Kenya to gather information for my stories.

During this first year at Kijabe our son Jeffrey was born, on August 29, 1973. During that time another missionary and fellow RVA graduate, Tim Davis, asked me to travel to Churo in East Pokot with him. On that medical and evangelistic safari we took Nurse Sylvia Kinsman who held a clinic on the Saturday. Tim preached on Sunday and we returned to Kijabe Sunday night. AIM church work started in that area when Tim began visiting this little primary school in Churo in the early 1970s.

The next month Tim asked me go on another trip and also if I would consider taking over these monthly safaris when he and his family went on furlough in June. I agreed to do that for him.

Tim had resurrected a small primary school at Churo in 1970. For 200/ shillings or $30 per month, he provided for the needs of the school. He could buy a bag of *posho* (ground maize) for 30/ a bag from Laikipia farm manager Colin Francombe. Sugar and tea cost 40/ as well as 130/ for salaries for the two teachers. I took over this 'whopping bill' from June 1973 onwards.

Churo first appeared on AIM's list of areas to be reached with the Gospel in 1917, then again in 1946. For 25 years Tom Collins, a veteran AIM missionary, had walked through Pokot from other mission stations where he lived with his wife Ruth (neé Barnett)—Tambach, Kabartonjo, Nginyang. In 1964, at the end of his life, he told his mission leader and brother-in-law Erik Barnett that he reckoned in all his time in Pokot perhaps only two people had believed in Jesus Christ. Tom had learned the language, helped to translate the New Testament, and spent many hours and days walking with the Pokot warriors, spending nights in their huts. During our early years in Pokot, Tom was well-remembered. "What you're telling us must be true," we were told many times, "because that's what *Bwana Kolong* told us."

We only owned a small Toyota Corolla station wagon in those days (a gift from our home church, Bethel EC in Conestoga, PA). But John Dykes, who owned Marmar Ranch, let us use his Land Rover to go to Churo. Then on one safari, Dr. Paul Jorden, a one year volunteer orthopedic surgeon at Kijabe Medical Hospital and author of **Surgeon on Safari**, offered to buy a second-hand Land Rover for us. We went to Churo with Dr. Jorden several times and on one occasion he took his wife Janet and most of their nine children with them. With his large family, Dr. Jorden was a 'real Pokot man!'

During our early trips to Churo it was still a wild and unspoiled place in East Pokot. We would meet elephant or buffalo on the way in through the Laikipia Ranch adjacent to Pokot. We also saw lion on occasion. While sleeping in the open on the primary school compound at Churo, we would hear hyena at night, and sometimes lion. One morning we found leopard tracks in camp.

Hearing these sounds reminded me of an interesting experience in the Suswa area in 1973 with Dr. John Stauffer, a long time friend and journalism professor who was visiting from the States with his wife, Patty. It was dusk on the dry plains behind Suswa volcano in the Great Rift Valley of Kenya. We had set up our tents in a dry riverbed under the shade of a lovely expansive acacia tree. The sun had just dipped behind the Maasai Hills. Hues of red, purple and dark gray intensified their colors as the minutes went by until it all went dark.

Earlier in the day we had shot a kongoni antelope with a fine set of horns. We now tied it up in a nearby tree to encourage some exciting nighttime action. We cooked a meal over a campfire. Drinks were served on a camp table and we sat back to enjoy one of the great pleasures of the African wild. Hyenas made a few of their signature calls. Jackals yapped nearby. But we wanted the King of the Beasts, the massive African black-maned lion to show himself that night.

Darkness comes quickly in the African night and with it a spectacular display of myriads of sparkling stars. As we dined under the stars, the spreading acacias were silhouetted against the skyline. No houses or signs of civilization could be seen or heard. Even the nearest Maasai *boma* was at least 10 miles away. This was a taste of 'Old Africa,' unspoiled by man.

We waited until 11 pm to see if the lions we now heard would come. But their distant grunts didn't come closer. Finally, tired and weary, we turned in for the night and slept soundly. At daybreak John and I stepped outside our tents to see if the bait was still there. To our immense surprise and chagrin, there was nothing left in the tree—only lion footprints and a long drag mark down the riverbed!

In March 1975 church leaders from the Nakuru and Kijabe region came to our house at Kijabe to request us to be fulltime missionaries in Pokot. They were sending one of their national pastors there but he needed a supporting missionary to live in the area as well.

January 1976 found us moving to Amaya to begin work on a mission station there. Mary Ellen's parents came to visit, and her Dad, Dave Huber, built a house for the pastor at Churo. Kent Davis, an engineer living at Kijabe, together with his wife Beth, also helped out, and Kent transported Rev. Samuel Njau and his family to Churo in July 1976.

During the months of building, we lived in tents along the Amaya River. We enjoyed the wildlife and often had freshly killed antelope or buffalo for the table. On Easter Sunday we enjoyed guinea fowl stew.

While we were on furlough, Kent Davis and Dr. Jim Propst had installed a water ram and pipeline from the Amaya River to the station at Amaya. This was a real blessing for our building work. In June 1976 we officially moved from the Literature Department at Kijabe to our new work at Amaya among the Pokot people. Kent and

Beth helped us move to our tented location at Amaya. We completed construction of the pre-fabricated house Kent had designed at Kijabe and had transported to Amaya with a Diguna lorry.

When we went to live among the Pokot in the middle 1970s, the women were covered in bangles and beads and wore only necklaces for covering above the waist. The girls were all being circumcised. An African missionary, Rev. Samuel M. Njau, who left the comforts of his own land and people to work among a hostile tribe and live in harsh conditions, said this, "If only one Pokot comes to believe in Jesus Christ as his Savior, it is worth all our time and effort here." Pastor Njau with his wife Ruth and their children lived and ministered among the Pokot people for 15 years and saw hundreds of Pokot become Christians and dozens trained in their weekly Bible studies.

Pastor Samuel had no problem confronting the pagan culture head on. Having learned from the disastrous impact pagan culture had on his own people, his parents, grandparents, and their families, he immediately went about protecting the young Pokot girls of the Christian mothers.

Pastor Njau together with his wife Ruth took such young girls into their own home, later sending them outside the area to stay with strong Christian families. The girls attended boarding schools, with the pastor and his wife somehow managing to help with their fees. When Pokot women made professions of faith in Christ, he insisted they remove all their beads and bangles and cut their hair, which was corn curls covered in ashes and grease, telling them that those adornments represented pagan elements of their culture.

I should hasten to add that these changes were not affected early on, but only after the Njaus had been there many months and even years, befriending the Pokot, teaching them the Word of God and listening to what the new church elders advised about the pagan aspects of their culture. Significantly, making these drastic changes was very effective in keeping these women from returning to their dances, beer making, and traditional ceremonies.

Paulo Namunyan (now deceased), an older Pokot man, was one of the first genuine converts to Christ; he helped Rev. Njau understand the cultural insights of his people. Paulo was considered a worthless fellow by his fellow Pokot. He had even been jailed for stealing cows from another tribe. In an interesting twist, it was when he was in prison in Mariakani that he learned to read; an invaluable skill when he became a Christian and evangelist in the Churo area. He had lost all the money from the sale of those stolen cows in an unsuccessful bar business. He was sometimes called a monkey for stealing food from people's gardens.

But when he became a Christian, Paulo was a different person. His words were taken seriously in the tribal councils. He earned respect from Pokot leaders by becoming an assistant to Pastor Njau and working together with him on farming—a new concept to these nomadic cattle people, but a concept that gained quick acceptance. It not only provided maize, the mainstay of their diet, but it was something the neighboring enemy tribes could not steal—their land or their acres of crops.

For a couple years, there was a big increase in church membership and scores of men and women turned to Christ and away from worshiping and revering their elders, mountains, cows and stars.

Paulo, Yohana, and Julius (two other converts) learned from experience early on that they too could not continue attending pagan ceremonies and heathen rituals. There was a ceremony that many Pokot men attended to receive blessings from the old diviners, to pray to their gods for rain and to have their cattle blessed as well. These three men did not want to miss out on the roasted meat that would be served during the ceremony. They watched with disdain the empty rituals that were being performed. But they ate heartily when the slaughtered bull was served.

A final and key element of the ceremony is for the diviner to undress, walk around naked before the group, and call on his gods to bless them, sometimes spitting on those gathered as he passes by. When he came near the three Christians, Paulo said to the others, "We should leave; truly this is not good for us to be here."

As they walked away, the naked diviner shouted after them, "Why are you leaving before the blessing? You enjoyed the feast, now you must wait for the blessing." But the men hurried away.

When they got out of range of those at the ceremony they talked among themselves and agreed that it is not good for Christians to attend these ceremonies. They went back to Pastor Njau telling him what they had done. He immediately counseled them what the Word of God teaches concerning the importance of being separated from the old life and its heathen practices.

Unfortunately, many western missionaries have not taken seriously the importance of insisting that the traditional people completely separate themselves from the practices of their tribal culture that are pagan or against Scripture. Especially forbidden are those aspects that demand loyalty to the point of worship of the elders, ceremonies and rituals. We must confess that we erred on the side of expecting the Holy Spirit to convict the new believers about when to change concerning these issues in their lives, whereas Pastor Njau was absolutely right in obedience to Scripture and insisting on change.

When we were not insistent on change, the new Christians sometimes would freely participate in all church activities and ceremonies while at the same time continue in the tribal practices. And as shown in the book of Acts in the Bible, and in church history, when you are like Pastor Njau you suffer for it and your life can be threatened.

Four times the traditional Pokot attempted to kill Rev. Njau. After one of those attempts, four men who were involved were put in prison for attempted murder. Rev. Njau had an old station wagon Land Rover that he used in his ministry, as well as to transport his own family members to the bus stage at Mugie, 20 miles from Churo. One night around 10 pm, two former students from the primary school came to the Njau's house begging him to help friends who were injured in a vehicle accident 10 miles down the road. They even offered to pay for his help! For some reason Njau, who always was ready to help those who had a need and especially when they could pay for the use of his vehicle, did not feel he should go. "It was the Holy Spirit restraining me," Njau later told us.

And it was good he did not go, because these two young men in collusion with two others had planned to murder him once he was away from home. There was no car, no accident, but only their evil plan. Later, when this became known, the men were handed over to the police.

Early on, when the traditional elders saw that fewer female circumcisions meant a loss of income that comes with that practice, another attempt was made to get rid of Njaus.

One night around 8 pm, over 50 warriors and youth were incited to kill the pastor. At the time, Njau was in his house with his wife and small children. There were also four men representing the Regional Church office in their home.

The Pokot began throwing stones at the house and shouting abuses at the pastor. They asked him to come outside to talk with them, all the time making war cries and throwing stones at the tin roof and flimsy wooden walls of the house. The visiting church elders were very frightened, but as they prayed together, Njau experienced a deep sense of safety and assurance from God that all would be well. After perhaps a half hour of these threatening and scary attacks, the men suddenly ran off and disappeared. Later, Njau learned the group had heard of another incident taking place in the nearby town that had caused their abrupt departure. They never returned.

In retrospect, you realize that often the whole issue of changing culture and tradition is really about the loss of control, power and income.

The Apostle Paul faced this with the demon-possessed girl who "earned a great income for her masters." When she was delivered of the demons, these masters were no longer in control and had lost the source of their lucrative income (Acts 16). When given in its entirety, the Gospel will always cause a change when accepted by any non-Christian traditional group. Unfortunately in many places today it is accepted as simply another belief to add to existing belief and not to REPLACE existing beliefs. Hence there is no conflict and no change.

In our early days in Pokot, I was invited to observe parts of some ceremonies, but was also told to go away from others. Probably the most oppressive or dark feeling I ever experienced was at a ceremony at Kokwo Toto, an area that even today is clouded with dark and sinister characters and practices. Munyukit and two others had slaughtered a goat. They drank the warm blood right out of the carcass, and then they walked around the carcass emoting deep chants to their gods. They would stop every so often, grab some offal from the dead animal, and smear it on their chests and knees. This routine continued for fifteen or more minutes. At the end, they roasted the goat whole and ate it. I did not partake, but was able to capture everything that took place on my video camera. I distinctly remember feeling oppressed in my spirit, even as I taped this pagan ceremony.

Often we would see a Pokot diviner 'reading' the intestines of a goat, to learn if it was going to rain, or if the enemy Turkana tribe was planning to attack. The people really believed what they were told, but I found that only half the predictions I witnessed ever came close to what actually happened. One time I distinctly remember the diviner was so absolutely sure his prediction of rain was true that he put his seal on the prophecy by rubbing the goat dung on his chest. But the rain didn't come for another several months though I am certain the diviner had an explanation for it. But because we were just learning about their culture and traditions, we didn't try to stop any of their practices; rather we tried to learn about them and understand how and why they did things. It was only after several years of working there that we learned how locked into their traditions they really were.

As we lived among the Pokot at Amaya, it did not take long for me to see the tribal discrimination that existed. I learned it was hopeless to try to get justice for the Pokot. The Turkana raided Amaya in 1978 and a subsequent police operation resulted in many Pokot being beaten, raped and imprisoned. When the Pokot complained, the District Commissioner (DC) told them to travel to his office in Tangulbei, 15 miles away. But when they arrived that day the District Officer (a lower level official) told them it was necessary to travel to Marigat to meet the DC if they wanted to air their grievances.

I was not about to let these diversionary tactics stop me from seeing justice done for the Pokot, so I transported the group to

Marigat, 50 miles further on. The final straw was when the Inspector of Police in Marigat told us we had to go even further, to Kabarnet, the District Headquarters, to find the elusive DC. This was yet another 25 miles.

Upon reaching Kabarnet we learned the DC was mysteriously "away on urgent business." When I spoke to the DO who was on duty he instructed me to take the group of Pokot to the head of police in Kabarnet.

Finally, I thought, we will certainly be able to see justice done now!

But the first thing the Inspector of Police asked me was, "Why are you bringing these murderers here?" as he pointed to Naibor, one of the men in the group. Naibor, who was in his 70s, had not been on a raid in years. Others in the group included two of his wives and several other abused Pokot.

I was livid with disgust for the official government security representative to be so insensitive to many innocent people who had been mistreated.

"Is it right to charge a man as guilty before he has even been tried?" I asked with a raised and controlled voice.

"No, you're right," he replied. "But go back to the District Officer and he'll explain things to you in the right manner." The DO then took great pains to tell me how the government knew what they were doing; they knew who the bad guys were and it had not been wrong in punishing the people.

Later I found out from one of the Pokot Christians that Naibor's bad reputation was somewhat deserved. He was the one who authorized raids and said the Pokot ritualistic prayers for blessing before the warriors went into battle.

Doubtless after that, there was a feeling among some government officials that "this missionary is interfering in internal matters that are not his business."

In fact, within a few months the Turkana raided Amaya again. We had been woken up by the gunfire and at 6 am I saw a Turkana man go by our house carrying a gun. Within a half hour, I called the Maralal police station on our two-way radio to alert them that the Turkana had raided and stolen hundreds of cattle (it turned out to be over 3,000). We had called at 6.30 am, but the two Land Rovers full of police did not arrive until 12.30 pm. It is normally a one hour drive from Maralal to Amaya. I drove my Toyota Land Cruiser pickup full of Pokot warriors and the vehicles had to stop where the road ended after about seven miles. When the 24 police and men later returned, the DC himself came down to congratulate his men. The DC told me the police had caught up to the Turkana, engaged them in battle, "killing over 60 of them" and retrieved all the 3,000 head of cattle.

That very same day Apawoi, our Chief, and Kamario, another Pokot who lived in the area, told me this story: "We reached the Turkana about five in the evening," Apewoi said. "We wanted to attack immediately and get our cows back. But the police said it was better to sleep and very early the next morning we could make the attack. But at 5 am some police shot flares over the Turkana encampment to warn them and all the 'Turks' fled, leaving the cattle behind."

Kamario, one of the early professing Christians during the Davis's ministry among the Pokot, and their neighbor at both Amaya and Orus. He moved when the Davis family moved.

"We didn't even kill one Turkana," Kamario said with disgust. "But at least we got our cattle back." Two days later the newspaper account related that the police had recovered 3,000 cows and killed more than 60 Turkana.

Over the next few weeks, we heard rumors that the DC was trying to move us out of Amaya. A good American friend who spoke Samburu fluently had heard this report from the Samburu, who said the DC wanted us out and our friends out as well. The Samburu told our friend these government officials were using the Turkana to steal cows from Pokot and Samburu and then would resell them across the border of Uganda. These officials doubtless felt we were aware of their corrupt activities.

The other family soon was expelled from Samburu and went to live in Rumuruti, not too far away.

Fortunately for us, a couple months later, after the first President of Kenya had passed away, the new President transferred many of the government officials to serve in different locations. The District Commissioner of Samburu was moved, and the local District Officer retired. So we carried on in our work peacefully, without further fears of political interference.

After these events the church work began to expand. The mission assigned Ruth Ewert, an adventurous Canadian nurse, to Amaya and she developed the medical work. The raids became less frequent and began to occur further away from Amaya at a place called Orus, where we later moved and began ministry in January 1985.

We also benefited from our friendship with the Catholic priest from Maralal who was in charge of the Samburu side of Amaya. We invited Father Taloni to our home for meals and shared our American imported 'goodies' with him. Later, he sent us a goat as a gift. It was not long before those on the board of the Amaya Primary School were mostly our AIC men, including the chairman. Whenever we would visit Maralal, we would stop to greet Father Taloni and we remain friends to this day.

Pray for the Pokot Clinic in Kenya

**Take a New Step Forward That Will
JAR YOU LOOSE
AND CHANGE YOUR LIFE
Your Change will help to build a permanent clinic for 10,000
Pokot!**

The Art Davis Family

The Art Davis family prayer card from 1987.

When we lived at Amaya in the early 1980s Dr. Paul Jorden, a good friend and supporter, came to visit us. One morning we were informed that a very sick boy was being brought to the dispensary and there was a request for Dr. Jorden to examine the boy.

Upon reaching the dispensary, we discovered that not only was the boy dead, but he had been dead for some time. As best as Doc Jorden could tell, there was no evidence of any wound, sickness, or anything that had caused the death of this 'healthy' looking

15-year-old. Only later did we learn that the boy had been cursed and actually died of fear.

That reminds me of another corpse that had to be dealt with by someone outside the family. It is so sad when family members are not there to usher the relative to his eternal home through decent, proper and respectful handling.

Peter McCallum, AIM missionary from 1965-2000, came to visit us at Amaya in East Pokot in 1980. Word came to us early one morning that a Pokot had died as his friends were bringing him to the mission dispensary. In Pokot culture it is taboo to touch a dead body, so the Pokot left him in the bush and some passersby came and told us about it. Peter and I went with *jembes* (hoes) and shovels, dug a shallow grave, buried the man and put a mound of stones on top.

Close Calls With Death

We not only saw death around us, we personally faced death on several occasions. No doubt the longest most drawn out close call with death occurred during the 1982 attempted coup in Kenya. Again, I was with good friends John and Patty Stauffer. We had left Nairobi to climb the highest peak in the Aberdare mountain range. On Saturday, July 31, we reached 10,000 feet and spent the night in a Kenya Wildlife Service *banda*.

But in the middle of the night, John developed stomach cramps and upset stomach. He had scaled the tops of Mt. Kenya and Mt. Kilimanjaro before, so did not think it was altitude sickness. But by 4 am he was so uncomfortable that we decided to pack up and drive down early. We left about 5 am and when we reached a lower altitude, he immediately felt better.

We drove to the Aberdare Country Club to enjoy a good breakfast, and then planned to drive back to Nairobi where we were living at the time. As we went to reception to inquire about breakfast, the receptionist said very tersely, "You cannot move." John, still feeling a bit wiped out from being sick in the night, was not humored. He assured her he could move and showed his arms moving up and down.

"No," she replied. "There has been a coup," (pronouncing the 'p' with a hard sound). We began asking others and soon learned the Kenya Air Force had seized the main broadcasting station in Nairobi and some other key installations. People were staying close to the radio to hear the news. At 10 am we heard the coup had been put down and the government was again in control. "You may now move about normally," the broadcaster concluded.

We decided to wait at least an hour before going down to Nairobi. The next news broadcast again made things sound normal, so we decided to leave for Nairobi around noon. As we traveled south on the highway, we saw very few other vehicles. Any cars coming from the direction of Nairobi flashed their headlights and some gave hand signals, telling us to turn around.

But as we saw no problems, we continued driving. When we reached the Kahawa army barracks, about 10 miles east of Nairobi, we were stopped and told to get out of the car to be identified. As we were being searched, one officer was a bit too personal in his search of Patty; her husband, John, gave him a strong shove backwards and he skidded off the loose gravel on the road's shoulder and fell down a few feet to the field below. He came back up cursing and with his pistol drawn. Fortunately, a superior officer came over quickly and calmed him down.

When we asked about continuing on to Nairobi, the commander assured us there were no problems and gave us the go ahead. In less than a mile, we were stopped again and gave identification. When the officer saw our address on the side door of the Land Rover was Nyahururu, he asked if we knew Father John. I said I had heard of him and we were given permission to move on.

My Land Rover was a dull green color with a canvas back so it looked like a military vehicle. We felt this aroused suspicions. The coup had been staged by the air force and the government was defending itself with the army. Throughout the day cars full of air force soldiers would drive up to an army-controlled roundabout, shoot all the soldiers and then take over that roundabout. Then vehicles carrying army soldiers would drive up, shoot the air force men, and take back the roundabout.

As we approached the city, we were stopped again at the St. Stephen's ACK Church roundabout. John and Patty were ordered out of the vehicle and told to put their hands on their heads and walk the 500 feet to the grass in the middle of the roundabout. I was instructed to follow them slowly in the vehicle. There were armed men barely visible in the deep storm drains along the road. They were firing at some apartments to our right. I could see guns sticking out of some windows returning fire. I got out of the car at the roundabout and walked over to John and Patty. An army colonel scolded us for driving around in the middle of a coup. As I was apologizing, the colonel looked toward where Forest Road joins the roundabout. "Get down!" he shouted, as a black Mercedes sedan sped toward us. We complied and lay flat, but there was little cover in the sparse grass growing under the shade trees. Automatic weapons fire came over our heads from the right, and the Mercedes went into a drainage ditch, its right side front and rear tires spinning in the air. The colonel immediately told us to 'move' and we drove on toward Westlands and the safety of a flat (apartment) belonging to some missionary friends.

At the Westlands roundabout we saw a police station wagon with guns sticking out of every window and the uplifted rear door. As they saw us go through the roundabout, they followed and ordered us to stop. They had been holding about 500 looters at bay, all poised to break into stores during the turmoil. I was told to get out on my side and John and Patty were on the other. While I was showing identification, John was having a confrontation with a uniformed policeman who propped the muzzle of an AK-47 on John's chest and said, "Give me your money!" After the morning he'd had so far, John's good nature began to fade. So instead of complying, he yelled for the entire world to hear, "Art, this policeman wants my money!"

That caught the attention of the head policeman on my side of the car, who ran around and ordered his men not to take anything. So John saved the $100 he had left in his left blue jean pocket and we were released to drive the last quarter mile to our friends.

Mary Ellen and the kids were across town in the rented flat that was our home for those two years we were assigned to work in Nairobi. As that house had no phone, I called the Mayfield Guest House and Chuck Kinzer very kindly drove several blocks to tell her where we were and that we were okay. She had no idea what we had been through. In fact, she was relieved we were climbing a mountain in the Aberdares, far from all the trouble of the city, not knowing we had come down early because of John's illness.

That morning she and the kids had driven to AIC Ngong Road, the church we attended, about one mile away, only to find the church gate was closed and locked. Someone eventually came to the gate to say there was no service taking place that day. She remembers hearing what she thought were firecrackers going off throughout the day, but since we were in the same area as the Langata army barracks, she thought it was just normal practice. We had no TV or radio either. Finally, early in the afternoon our Sri Lankan neighbors told her a bit of what was happening throughout the city.

When we finally arrived home on Monday morning, things had quieted down, but we had to postpone our scheduled trip to Mombasa as we did not feel it was really safe yet to be on the highways.

My brother Van also had a dramatic escape from death during that period. He used a 40-foot ocean going catamaran with sails called *Tafuta Tu* to take the Gospel to the archipelago islands in the Lamu area of Kenya's north coast. Certain repairs could only be done at a boat yard located in the small fishing village of Kipini, located on the mouth of the Tana River about 40 miles away by sea. Van had made this sea trip to Lamu and the adjoining islands on several occasions and so was familiar with the passage and its limited navigational aids.

On the day before he set off on another sailing voyage in May 1981, Van had taught a lesson on faith at the St. Andrews Anglican Church at the interdenominational service he and Kathy had helped to start in Malindi.

The next day, Monday afternoon, was a high spring tide and Van with five others slipped off the moorings, raised sail and made their way through a natural cut in the reef from the Silversands Beach anchorage and set a course northward toward Kipini, a straight run of just over 40 miles. They hoped by early morning to make the approach to the only navigational light at Kipini at a high tide. On board were three other Europeans and two Africans (resident seamen from Kipini).

With full sails of main and jib and the wind barely at five knots the going was at first very slow and the wind was not blowing the usual afternoon pattern. As the sun went down, and the full moon appeared over the horizon they enjoyed a sumptuous evening meal sitting at a table on the spacious space just aft of the cock pit.

As the night moved in, the wind picked up considerably, and the moon shone like a floodlight; the sailing was a true sailor's paradise. Van and Alex took the responsibility to navigate and operate *Tafuta Tu* through the night, and the African crew would take over to navigate the vessel in the morning in their familiar home village waters of Kipini. The cabin beds were all made up, but everyone opted to sleep out on the decks—much cooler than in the cabins.

During the night all went very well and time went by quickly. As dawn broke Tuesday morning they found themselves and *Tafuta Tu* in serious trouble as they made the approach to the mouth of the Tana River. It was about 6.20 am and they were sinking! They attempted to turn the craft into the wind. Van went down into the cabin and collected all the life vests. Others emptied the jerry cans of petrol into the sea, freeing up buoyancy devices on which to hang, another took a knife and cut some of the sail sheets. When all this was completed, the unexpected happened. As Van came up out of the cabin area a large swell came over the stern of the vessel and swamped the starboard side of the ship causing it to turn turtle so slowly they were able to crawl along the side to the bottom of the hulls. At the same time 10 jerry tins and the ropes were all lashed together and secured to the boat.

Once on the hull they seated themselves on one of the two skegs (a 10 ft x 2 x 12 hardwood timber bolted through the keel on the center of each hull to give better handling qualities). While seated there, various bit and pieces began making their way up from the interior of the boat. The first thing Van retrieved from the water was his pocket New Testament—hardly soaked or damaged. Van remarked, "Well friends, we shall certainly be needing this before this day is over!" The next item they retrieved from the water was a four-inch water-soaked foam mattress, which they laid over the skeg to make their sitting on the two inches a lot more comfortable. Then one of the spare sails surfaced which they attempted to use as a sail. They estimated the boat was two to three miles off the south shore of Kipini.

Thankfully it was a very overcast day with frequent rain squalls, which provided fresh drinking water. However, when the squalls came up the wind and rain caused the sea to break over the up-turned vessel; the powerful waves washed them into the sea. They suffered cuts on their arms and legs from the barnacles on the hull when they climbed back on. Land was visible and gave them hope.

About 3 pm the top of the 30-foot mast began to hit the ocean floor. They feared there could be serious breaking up of the vessel that would put them in further danger. They decided to abandon ship; each person carrying a jerry tin as additional security and all 10 jerry tins were roped together. Before leaving the boat, Van took out the pocket New Testament and read five pertinent verses in the account of the Apostle Paul in his shipwreck experience found in Acts 27:22-26. "Be of good cheer for I believe God . . ." Following the reading, Van led the group in prayer after which they abandoned ship.

As the party of six made their way toward shore they decided two of the party should make a strong swim for shore with a hope of getting help before sundown. They made it in good time with the help of the incoming tide and wind. Two of the four left on the sea had spent the whole previous night awake navigating and manning the vessel: Van and Alex. They were beat! It was a real effort for them to keep their legs moving constantly, plus keeping a kind of balance on the jerry tin. Night soon came upon them and the moon shone brightly, but now the tide was reversing direction; the winds were strong and they made little headway toward shore floating on their tins.

At some point during the early night hours one of the members suddenly became very hysterical, fearing drowning, and Van went to his side to assist and comfort him, but while doing this Van's life line to the rest became detached, and Van found himself being carried away from the group by the current, wind and tide. As Van moved away quickly from the group, the words from Alex's wife Sally were, "Van, whatever you do—DO NOT FALL ASLEEP, if you do YOU WILL NOT WAKE UP ALIVE!"

Van recalls singing all the hymns and choruses he could recall and praying, while he struggled to stay afloat on the jerry can. After many hours he suddenly found himself being rocketed by a large wave that landed him on the South Kipini Beach. He had no strength left in his legs so he dug in with his elbows to escape the forces of the incoming spring tide. He later learned the time was about 2 am. He suddenly heard voices shouting in Swahili "*Ndiyo huyu, Ndiyo huyu—yeye yu hai, yeye yu hai*! It's him, it's him—he's alive, he's alive!"

He was given a dry shirt, wrapped in a blanket and placed on a motorbike that carried him to the banks of the Tana River from where he was carried across in a local dugout canoe. He was then taken to the home where the other members of the shipwreck were, all alive and well. They slept and had breakfast. Some of the local fishermen brought them a piece of the *Tafuta Tu*. This was part of the board that went across the top of the wheel house area on which Van had put a ceramic plaque with the verse from Proverbs 3:5,6. "Trust in the Lord with all your heart and lean not unto thine own understanding. In all thy ways acknowledge Him and He shall direct thy paths."

A Power Confrontation

After our interlude in Nairobi we returned to our work among the Pokot people of Baringo District. In 1985 we moved to another area called Orus. There we lived in tents for 18 months, moving to three locations while we searched for water.

We witnessed an amazing power confrontation in 1985 between Alemongora, a powerful diviner, and his diminutive third wife, Mama Cheptaran, the mother of two small children. She came to church as a result of visits we had made to her village, together with Evangelist Reuben. Within six months of hearing the Word of God every Sunday and at other times in her village, she believed "it was really true" and professed her faith in Christ. Six weeks later her husband Alemongora, a respected diviner, began the ceremonies to protect the village from sicknesses that normally come after the onset of the rains. As he approached Mama Cheptaran she politely but firmly refused to have the goat skin charm put on her upper arm or on those of her children. "Jesus will protect me," she declared.

Those were blasphemous words to her husband! He immediately got angry and insisted on attaching the charm to her arm. As she continued to adamantly resist, he decided on another course of action. Leaving the thin goat skin bands with Mama Cheptaran, Alemongora told her he would go to the others in the village to put the charms on them. "When I return," he threatened her, "if you and the children are not wearing the charms I will beat you very severely."

Mama Cheptaran prayed fervently that Jesus would protect her, not just from any sicknesses, but from her husband's severe beatings, which she had experienced in the past. When her husband returned sometime later, Mama Cheptaran expected the worst. But God had miraculously overruled Alemongora's angry spirit; he had not given up on his determination to show his power over that of Jesus, but decided on a more subtle approach. "Since you refuse to wear the charms," he stated, "we will all be watching you for the next weeks. If you get sick it will show that Jesus doesn't have power and you will come to fear and obey our traditions and the power of the elders."

Immediately Mama Cheptaran came to Reuben and us, telling about her dilemma. Over the next few weeks Christians at Orus and other places prayed earnestly for her safety and good health. During that time some in the village did get sick, some quite seriously. But Mama Cheptaran and her daughters remained healthy and well.

This power confrontation strengthened the faith of Mama Cheptaran and the other new believers tremendously. But it also angered her husband and the other elders. Alemongora would try several more times to defeat the power of Jesus in the life of his wife.

The next incident occurred when she gave birth to another child a couple years later. At just a few weeks of age, this baby son became very ill and died; Mama Cheptaran was on her way with the baby to a dispensary five miles away when he died. She dug a shallow grave and buried the baby by herself. Alemongora, of course, attributed the death to his wife's refusal to allow him to perform some healing arts from his goat sacrifices on the child.

But the worst offense in his view and one, totally against traditional culture was that Mama Cheptaran came to the church service the following Sunday. In Pokot tradition, when a person touches a dead body, he or she must remain in isolation in the hut or village for one month. In great anger Alemongora came to the church group who were meeting under a shade tree and forcibly dragged his wife out, beating her mercilessly for not following the cultural rules. He used the Pokot stick called *likup* which has a sharp curved point at one end, intended to crack a skull open or gouge out chunks of flesh. He struck her several times and Mama Cheptaran today still bears the scars from that beating on her back and shoulders.

But Rebecca, the name Mama Cheptaran had taken when baptized, never wavered in her faith. In fact, another incident with Alemongora soon followed the death of this child. Evangelist Reuben and I went to console Rebecca on the loss of her baby. Alemongora was listening as we told Rebecca the baby was now in heaven with Jesus and that she would see him again. Alemongora flew into a rage, almost as if he were possessed. He shouted at us that no one will ever see the baby again, that there is no heaven and than no one can know what happens to the dead. Because of Alemongora's anger Reuben and I felt the wise thing was to leave, telling Rebecca we would return another day.

On the day we had planned to return I was called away to drive someone to the hospital. So Reuben, together with Paulo Tododong, another believer, went to the village. As they neared the dry riverbed close to Rebecca's village, she met them with a warning, "Don't come. My husband has hired four warriors to beat you up today." But Reuben was a fearless warrior in his bygone days, having faced rhino, buffalo and Turkana warriors. As he told Rebecca he was not afraid and would come anyway, she went ahead to their home to await their arrival.

When the two men reached the village, Reuben greeted Alemongora and the four warriors jovially, as if he knew nothing. After half an hour of talking about their cows and their families, the fact that the rains were late, where to take the herds for grass, etc, no one had made a move to attack Reuben and Paulo.

Finally one of the warriors pointedly asked Reuben, "What kind of charm are you wearing?"

Reuben replied, "I'm not wearing any charm. Why do you ask?"

They told Reuben they had been hired to assault him, but so far they had been unable to do anything. Therefore, they surmised he was wearing a very powerful charm. Showing them the New Testament he was carrying, Reuben explained that the most powerful force in the universe had stopped them from harming him. "The power you are looking for is not a charm, but a Person. His Name is Jesus Christ, the Son of God and it is His power that has protected us," Reuben told them. For the next hour Reuben and Paulo talked to the men about Jesus Christ and His power and His coming to earth to die for man's sins. That day none of the warriors present decided to follow Jesus, but they surely knew who Jesus was and the source of Reuben's power.

Several years later Cheptaran, the oldest daughter, was approaching the marriageable age of 11 or 12 years. Because her mother did not want Cheptaran to be circumcised, she secretly sent her to a Christian family in another village where she could attend school and receive Christian teaching. Again, she was beaten by her husband, who would have also whipped his daughter Cheptaran if he could have found her.

Cheptaran herself has the degree of determination that helped her mother! She enjoyed school, wearing the uniform with shoes, learning to read, knowing more about the world. She stayed safely in Churo for a few years but eventually came home where she lived at home and continued on in school, even against her father's wishes.

Several years later friends from First Baptist Church in Wayne, Michigan, kindly offered to sponsor Cheptaran, now baptized Evelyn, through high school. It wasn't until she had finished high school and was hired by the government to help with voter registration, that her father came to agree she had chosen a good path. Using most of the salary she had received for that short term job, Evelyn gave her father enough money to buy a cow. Now suddenly he was 'bragging' that in his village area only he had a daughter who had finished high school! Evelyn now has two children of her own. She inherited a great Christian legacy from her mother and they both have demonstrated the greater power of Jesus Christ over Pokot culture and traditions that simply venerate man's customs and cultures and not the One True God!

The Rain Story

When we surveyed the hot, dry and desolate area of Orus in January 1984, we were shocked by the desperate water needs. In one village we met a woman who had just walked four miles one way for water, waited her turn for hours, and then walked home over that hot, hostile, and lava rock landscape in the intense afternoon heat.

On a later trip there in February with Mary Ellen's sister, Shirley, and her husband, Bob Leaman, things were so bleak that Shirley commented, "I certainly hope you're not thinking of living here!" The local Pokot had just burned off the grass in preparation for the March rains and the raging fires had destroyed many of the thorn trees that provide shade. I remember seeing a monitor lizard skeleton still in its upright position under an ashy white burned-out bush.

When we arrived to live at Orus in January 1985, things were much worse as the rains hadn't come in 1984 and now the sky was still barren of clouds. Pokot diviners had spent days imploring their gods for rain, all to no avail.

I was driving two hours one way on a very rough road out to Tangulbei a couple times weekly to fill half a dozen plastic jerry cans at the government borehole. The Pokot and their calves and young goats waited their turn for hours, some through the night, for their chance to drink a little bit of water from the Orus spring, which yielded a paltry 200 liters an hour at best.

Cows and fully-grown goats were being taken 15 miles to Tangulbei, to the Amaya River, or even further to the Mukutani River for water. By March of 1985, many animals had died or were suffering from lack of water.

On March 17, 1985 (Mary Ellen's Irish ancestry reminding us it was St Patrick's Day), we went to the thorn tree church as usual to talk about Jesus Christ to the Pokot. After every church service for the past 10 Sundays, we would have time for questions from the local people to learn about their culture and religion, as well as to explain to them the beliefs of Christianity.

On this particularly hot dry Sunday afternoon an old, tall, wiry Pokot man named Lorengelech stood up and said, "We have sacrificed our best animals and prayed at our holy mountains, but our god has not heard these prayers. He does not love us. He has thrown us away."

Then he pointed a long bony finger at me and asked, "Will your God answer a prayer for rain?"

Like a cowboy out West who has just seen a man draw his gun, I drew mine and fired.

"Sure," I answered, maybe too quickly!

"Then ask Him," the Pokot diviner challenged me.

Thoughts raced through my head. What if I pray and nothing happens? Will Jesus' Name be dishonored?

But in the same instant I felt the Holy Spirit saying very distinctively, "Pray and leave the results with God."

I told the 40 plus Pokot present that day, using Swahili and having Evangelist Reuben translate it into Pokot, that they must do two things. First, they must confess their sins, and then they needed to pray in Jesus' Name alone. The people all agreed and Reuben elaborated about sins that needed to be confessed: stealing cows, killing people, worshiping false gods.

When the people had agreed to the two things I had suggested, Lorengelech then added, "And let me also pray."

But Reuben and all the others quickly refused. Reuben told him, "You've just told us your god has not answered prayer so now we will pray in Jesus' Name alone."

I prayed in Swahili and Reuben translated what I said into Pokot. Then he also prayed in Pokot.

As in the days of Elijah, we expected to look up and see some cloud forming. But there was nothing but an intensely blue sky and bright sun.

That evening we visited the village of some warriors who had asked us to do tell them more about "this Jesus." We went to Domokwanyang's village on a bright starlit night. No clouds were visible anywhere. But the reward that night was that both Domokwanyang and his friend, Orioko, professed to put their trust in Christ as their Savior.

The next day we went on a trip to Nakuru, leaving early on a beautiful, clear, sunny morning. First we went 40 kilometers to our church leader's home at Churo, up in the hills. We spent a couple hours there, and then headed towards Nakuru.

As we came down the escarpment, we noticed a huge black cloud just over Orus and Orus only. We were thrilled and I said to Mary Ellen, "Maybe this is the rain we prayed for."

Three days later we returned on Thursday to our tent home at Orus and noticed mud on the road. The closer we got, the more we slipped and slid in the mud. On arrival we met a smiling Reuben with his wife, Esther. They were so happy and excited, telling us it had rained heavily on that Monday and every day since!

"In fact, we need to get into your tent and hold the poles up right now, as the wind and rain are so strong they knocked the tent down several times," Reuben told us as he looked at the sky.

We supported the tent poles for what seemed like a long time, but it was probably only 45 minutes. After the rain subsided, I let go and sat down on my camp cot bed—only to be surprised by a big gush of water coming out from under the mattress, where the water had gathered for the past three days.

But I was so tired and happy I didn't get upset. We just sat about emptying water from everywhere and trying to find a dry place in the camp to make a pot of tea.

The following Sunday, old Lorengelech stood up after the church service and told his people, "Truly, it is Jesus who has power with God."

About a dozen of those people present that Sunday made professions of faith in Jesus Christ. Sadly, Lorengelech was not one of them. And today we know of several of them who continue on in their faith in Jesus and have changed from believing in their ancestors and diviners as god to being faithful followers of Christ.

Lobonge's Story

True faith and a lasting testimony do not come easily in Pokot. One memorable example is that of Musa Lobonge. He was 16 when we met him and he became a good worker for us when we moved to Orus in 1985. Each morning before the start of work I would meet with the workmen for about an hour of Bible study and prayer. On most Sundays they would all come to the church. After about one year of this, the workers were down at the spring at Orus, cleaning and deepening it in order to allow more water to come forth and be saved in a small reservoir pond.

During their lunch break, Tododong, one of the workers who had major scars on his back and a deformed upper left arm from a fight with a buffalo a year earlier, stood up. He told the other two workers—Lobonge and Sewareng—that they needed to follow Jesus and not just pretend to, thinking it would ensure they would keep their jobs with the missionaries.

"What do we need to do?" asked Lobonge.

"We must remove our mudpacks, ear rings and necklaces," Tododong said, "and we must do what the Bible teaches."

Later that day they borrowed a pair of scissors from Mama Jeff (Mary Ellen), cut off their mudpacks with all the underlying hair, shaved their heads and washed their scalps clean. Then they announced to Evangelist Reuben and me that now they had truly become Christians.

For the first few months these three men showed more interest at the Bible study and in church and the things of the Bible. We were very happy and encouraged them. But then Lobonge, as per Pokot custom, began the cultural practice of having sex with the young girls. Reuben confronted him, telling him that from a biblical standpoint this was wrong, and Lobonge repented.

Pokot girls dressed up for a circumcision ceremony in 2000.

Then Lobonge was in line for the next age grade to begin the process to go through the circumcision ceremony. Charles, evangelist at Kokwo Toto, and Zakayo, the mature Christian nurse working there, advised Lobonge against following the traditional route. They prayed with him and counseled him regularly.

On the day of the start of the ceremony, Lobonge spent an hour with Zakayo and they prayed together. As he left Zakayo's compound, Lobonge headed in the direction of Charles' house to have tea and pray with him. But while walking the 100 yards between the two houses, Lobonge veered off and instead headed to the ceremonies. He later told us a 'strong spirit' came over him, compelling him to go several miles away to where the ceremonies were taking place.

Things that are done at these ceremonies are immoral, degrading and full of pagan prayers to the dead, the cows, etc.

Two months later, when the ceremonies were completed, Lobonge came home. The first thing he did was to come to the church elders and confess his sins of attending the ceremonies. "I feel absolutely dirty," he told the church elders, "and need to be cleansed."

They prayed with him, telling him he would be under church discipline for six months, after which he should plan for baptism, taking a name from the Bible to show he was permanently choosing a new way of life and a new faith. Lobonge quickly agreed to that.

For the past 20 years, Musa Lobonge has stood firm in his faith. He married Cheptamu, a very beautiful Pokot girl, who came to Christ immediately. She chose the name 'Grace' when she was later baptized. When a son marries, and especially the firstborn, custom is that the father gives him a good share of his own herd of cattle, goats and sheep. Lobonge's father Limongora was so angry that for several years he refused Musa his traditional startup herd. Limongora even cursed the couple so that they would never bear children.

Grace Lobonge, now the wife of evangelist Musa Lobonge, at the first water well in the Orus area in 1986.

Because Lobonge was the oldest son of Limongora, he was expected to follow in his father's footsteps to become the next 'head diviner' of the area. Limongora earlier thought he had won a victory when 'the spirits' had led Lobonge to the circumcision ceremony.

As the years passed and Musa turned out to be an outstanding son, father, church elder and businessman (his wife bore him many sons, nine by now), Limongora relented and gave him his share of cattle and goats that had been withheld from him because of his Christian testimony.

Lobonge has become a strong evangelist for the church and is a testimony to the Pokot community around him. His God-given business acumen has enabled him to own the most successful *duka* (local shop) in all of Kokwo Toto. His herds have increased in size. His older sons are attending school and the oldest completed high school in 2009. Musa has built a sturdy and permanent house for his family and has bought a pickup truck. He has never asked the missionaries or the church for any financial support and God's hand of blessing is obviously upon him and his family. His father is now proud of him; the other sons waste their wealth on the local beer. But it has taken over 20 long years for him to establish his testimony.

The Churo High School Story

We first met Namunyan in January 1973 on a visit to the Churo Primary School with missionary Tim Davis. Paulo Namunyan was one of the poorest men in Pokot. In his earlier life he was called a 'monkey' because he scrounged for food in others' gardens. He had also been notorious for squandering money by drinking the local brew to excess. He was a cattle thief, raiding other tribes to increase his herd.

But on one raid on the neighboring European ranch at Lonyiek, he was caught with several others and put in jail far from home at Makinnon Road in Coast Province. While there, Namunyan learned to read and write. These skills were a huge asset when he later became a Christian and church leader and elder. At Kenya's Independence Day on December 12, 1963, he along with thousands of others was pardoned and released from prison.

He promptly returned home and opened a bar at Suguta Marmar in Samburu country, 30 kilometers from home. But he never made a profit! He drank his proceeds away with his friends. Before long he was back in Churo begging from his friends and stealing from others. He married a Turkana girl who had been stolen on a cattle raid, so he did not have to pay any dowry.

Tim Davis was sponsoring the fledgling Churo School that only boasted 15 students and two Christian teachers, whom Tim had brought in from outside the area. He had begun this help to Churo in 1970.

Tim had organized some men from Churo to be on the school committee and Namunyan was one of them. By this time Namunyan had heard the Gospel of eternal life through faith in Jesus Christ from

Tim and the teachers. But he continued his drinking habits with his friends, wasting any income he received on buying the local brew.

But slowly, over a period of time, the teachers continued to talk to him and others about what it means to believe in Jesus. Sometime in 1973 Namunyan made a profession of faith in Christ, though it took months for him to stop drinking.

When the Africa Inland Church sent a Kenyan missionary, Pastor Samuel Njau, to Churo in 1976, he took it upon himself to thoroughly train several of the newly converted men, Namunyan being one of them. Within a year he was baptized and took the name Paulo. Then he and his wife had a Christian wedding ceremony in the church. Now this despised 'ne'er do well' man who had been called a 'monkey' became a leading responsible leader in the community and an evangelist of the church.

Chepunya, the older girl in this picture, was kicked in the head by a camel when she was about six years old. The blow fractured her skull leaving her unconscious for two weeks. The Davises took her to a hospital in Nakuru and she recovered fully.

In 1988 we tried to start a Christian high school in Churo, in East Pokot. One work team, led by Vince Peranunzi from San Diego, California, and hosted by Ray and Jill Davis, built the foundation and floor of the principal's house. The community had donated 100 acres for the school.

The following year, a second team led by long-term AIM missionaries Jerry and Annie Rineer built the first classroom.

A third team from John Brown University and headed by Dr. Kent and Beth Davis finished the classroom and started the chapel for the school and community. Each of those teams brought their own funding.

For the next three years no other teams came and no other funds came in. The school was left uncompleted. At a Divisional Development Committee meeting held in Tangulbei in February 1994 the government officer suggested that the Catholic mission take over the school as they had the funds to do the job.

Immediately Paulo Namunyan stood up to object. In faith he said, "Our church will build this school. Just give us more time."

Soon after that I had 'a chance' meeting with Paul Land, a visiting Christian businessman from Michigan, at the Mayfield Guesthouse in Nairobi. I was working with Evangelism Explosion as Director for East Africa at the time and had dropped by the guesthouse looking for friends and fellowship.

As I passed by a white-haired gentleman looking at a map of Kenya hanging on a wall, he turned and asked me, "Do you know where I can build a Christian high school?"

Two days later, Paul Land and I flew to the Mugie Ranch airstrip where my brother Ray was waiting with his vehicle, and we drove to Churo. (Ray and Jill had been assigned to Amaya following our assignment to Nairobi and the Africa Inland Church Missionary Board in 1982). At Churo we met with the elders and saw the plan Ray and an engineer had drawn up with the help of someone on an earlier work team.

That afternoon in the lone-standing classroom, Paul Land promised the church, community leaders and us missionaries that he would provide funding for the construction of a Christian high school at Churo!

Since the school began in 1995, over 200 students have made professions of faith in Christ because of the Bible teaching they received there. The school is now staffed by nationals, but in the early years we were helped and encouraged by many others. Henry and Lois Hildebrandt graciously consented to come from their retirement in Canada to supervise the construction of the buildings (even after being wakened by my call in the middle of their Canadian night). They had worked in Ukambani when I was a teenage boy; I knew them well and had gone on many hunts with Henry. Henry is a *'fundi'* (expert) at building and the facilities there today are a tribute to his skill and hard work. Lois wore many hats—keeping books and financial records, hosting visitors and short term workers, and keeping things running smoothly.

Art Davis receives a spear as an honor at the first graduation of Churo High School 1999, presented by Pastor Symon Kiuta.

Henry Hildebrandt, who built Churo High School, receives a spear from a Pokot pastor at the same celebration.

Martel (now deceased) and Anna Jane Fennig who served with AIM for many years as educators, lived at Churo, putting together the teaching staff, equipment, materials, and everything else needed to open a secondary school. They were assisted by Dr. Rod and Brenda Redding. For a time Harold Wickman, who lived at Amaya with Linda, his missionary wife, kept the books and records.

Paul Land then asked Bill and Carolyn Overway to supervise the Churo High School, which they did admirably for several years, entering into the life of the church and the community.

Others came for short periods of time—some using their teaching skills, others volunteering as drivers or mechanics. In fact, that's how our son Jeff met his future wife Kate. Her aunt and uncle, Dr. Jan and Carol Fields, with their two daughters taught at the Churo School for a term in 2001; Kate and another young lady from Michigan came with them as volunteer teachers. Jeff was working in Watamu, made a visit to Churo at our request, and the rest as they say, is history!

Helicopter Opens New Areas

In 1975 as we were walking into the Amaya Valley with missionaries Dr. Chet Sakura and nurse Ruth Ewert, carrying two trunks of medical supplies, we had no idea that 20 years later we would be reaching far more remote places with a helicopter.

In our early years in Pokot we did most of the evangelism and Bible teaching by going on foot to the villages scattered around the Amaya Valley. Later, we built roads into remote areas like Kaptuya and Orus and visited villages by Land Rover. This enabled us to get to places more quickly and more frequently.

Finally, in the 1990s when we had established church centers at Churo, Amaya, Kaptuya and Orus, we were offered the use of a helicopter to go even further afield. Paul Land, who had donated our second well-drilling rig and had funded the Churo High School, asked me on one of his visits if we could use a helicopter to reach those still unreached. I replied, "Sure! We never thought of that, but we would love to try it." The helicopter enabled us to have an outreach to the north of the Rift Valley, a virtual no-man's land because of the past raiding between the Turkana and the Pokot.

Mary Ellen Davis (right) on a medical safari using the helicopter.

Helimission is a Swiss-based helicopter mission that has been used worldwide to take evangelists and medical people with the Gospel message to normally unreachable areas. They had been based in Kitale, Kenya, for about 20 years before we started using their services. Tom LeCompte was the pilot in the early 1990s when we began using the program. Marc Schmidtke took over from Tom and we had several years of very interesting safaris into remote areas, leaving evangelists in these hard-to-access areas for four days at a time. Places like Napukut, Lochogia, Cheparka and Chesaa in Pokot were reached with the Gospel. In Samburu we traveled to Ntepes, Nairimirimo and Ngare Narok and at each location built a church. Dr. J. L. Williams of New Directions sponsored much of that.

We continued with this monthly outreach program for 10 years. During that time, we started 26 preaching points and established 18 churches.

The helicopter helped the Davis family reach areas not easily accessible by road.

From Foot Safaris to Helicopters

Once a month pilot Marc Schmidtke flew to Orus from Kitale. He would then carry Pokot evangelists to several preaching points in the rugged Pokot mountains nearby. After that, we would fly to Samburu and take a couple teams out from there; this program continued for several years. Other pilots with Helimission included Matthias Reuter, Markus Lehmann and Guenter Stoehr.

We did not depend on the helicopter to do all our work in establishing churches. Near us at Orus there is a mountain called Paka, 5,500 feet high, and my children and I—and sometimes our visitors—climbed it on several occasions. Usually we went up to share the Good News of Jesus Christ with the Pokot who lived up there in the crater.

We saw where John Fowler of the British Church Missionary Society had in earlier times built water catchments to enable the Pokot to harvest the steam that would then turn into good drinking water. Brilliant! So we built a couple more catchments.

British geologists surveyed that mountain and several others in the area to learn the possibility of generating electricity from the steam jets. They estimated that Paka Mountain alone could generate 15 % of Kenya's total power needs. Amazing! This area is now being developed as a source of thermal electrical power for Kenya.

But when Helimission landed their helicopter near the top, the elders objected vehemently, saying their gods lived up there and they did not want their 'god mountain' tampered with. This was reinforced when they heard the high pitched 'beep, beep, beep' warning signal the chopper emits when taking off. They yelled that their "gods were asking for help and had been taken away by the chopper."

Art Davis, second from the left, on a helicopter safari.

Mountain climbing and overland foot safaris were some of the methods we used to have time to talk to Pokot warriors who normally didn't have time for the missionary's stories of God. As we rested, or drank tea, or set up camp for the night, or sat around the campfire at night, we had many chances to talk to them about Jesus Christ. And the Christian Pokot who went with us became good at sharing their faith in Christ and learned lots of new Bible stories from us.

Jeff, Karen and I decided to climb to the tops of all the peaks in the Nasokol (pointed) Mountain area of southeastern Turkana. One peak was impossible to climb but Jeremy West, a skilled helicopter pilot, put us on the top for a brief moment, just so we could say we had been to the top of all the peaks of the area.

One of the significant stories from the helicopter ministry occurred when Rev. Solomon Ngugi prayed for rain in the dry season at Ntepes, in Samburu country. Pastor Solomon went on nearly every monthly helicopter safari for three years. He helped to establish preaching centers in several places and a church was eventually built at Ntepes.

On his third trip to Ntepes, having seen dozens of people accept Christ on the first two trips, Solomon found the believers very discouraged. In fact, many did not even come to the gathering tree when Solomon and his helper were left off by the helicopter. When he finally found a couple men he asked them what the problem was.

"After you left the last time," they explained, "the witchdoctor came and put a string around all the corrals of those who believed in Jesus. He told us we would be cursed if we followed Jesus."

Solomon asked them to name the biggest problem facing the Samburu. "Lack of rain," they answered.

So Solomon told them, "Then we will pray for rain."

As he was still talking with the new believers, the witchdoctor walked up and began listening. When he heard Solomon tell the people they would now pray for rain he became very angry. "You can pray for rain," he said, "but I will go to that big rock over there and pray to the Samburu god."

It was high noon when Solomon prayed. By 4 pm it was pouring rain at Ntepes and all the people were giving praise to Jesus Christ.

Another time when we landed with Marc some Samburu brought a woman who had been bitten by a snake. She was frothing at the mouth, couldn't sit up and was very weak. Because of its effectiveness in treating victims of snake bite, Marc had brought along his 100,000 volt 'stun gun' and I used that on her. The first time she never felt the shock; after half an hour when I again applied it to her arm she jerked her hand away. Marc later flew her to Maralal where she was given an injection to guard against infection. That woman and her husband believed in Jesus that day and are now leaders in the church.

This was the start of the Ntepes church. As their numbers grew, an evangelist was assigned there; we dug a well and constructed a church. Today Evangelist Peter Lolkidinye still serves there.

On another trip with Evangelist Reuben Cherindis, we were surprised to run into some Turkana who were herding their animals at a place called Nasorot (a Turkana word meaning 'natural dam'). The herdsmen spoke Swahili so we talked with them about Jesus Christ.

At that time, in 1986, the grass was nearly waist high everywhere at Orus and all over the valley below us. So it wasn't long before word got out to both the Turkana and the Pokot that there was good grazing. For the next several years the two groups mixed together on their common border. The last cattle raid led by Turkana into Pokot had been in June 1984 when they raided Orus, killed four people and stole 1,000 head of cattle.

A prominent Turkana leader named Kanyuman came to live in the valley at a place called Nasokol (a Turkana word meaning 'pointed mountain').

Kanyuman had lived near Amaya in the 1970s and enjoyed great honor and favor with both the Pokot and Samburu. Even Colin Francombe, a friend of ours and manager of the Laikipia Ranch, used to visit him and buy cattle from him. Colin said Kanyuman was always a generous host and he enjoyed spending a couple nights in his *boma*. We too found the same hospitality.

On one occasion we had an overnight stay in his *boma* at Napukut with Dr. Kent Davis and a team of young men from John Brown University in Arkansas. Kanyuman served *chai*, tea rich with camel milk, on our arrival. As we sat and talked with him, he had his warriors prepare a fattened sheep for our dinner. We shared the Gospel with him and several of his 10 wives and 15 or so children.

In most African cultures it is a sign of blessing if it rains when visitors are present. Well, that night must have been the 'mother of all blessings' as it poured heavily throughout the hours of darkness. Almost every one of us in our tents complained of rain; Kanyuman's people, in their simple grass and stick huts were also drenched.

From Foot Safaris to Helicopters

The Turkana chieftain Kanyuman, a highly respected resident in Pokot and Turkana areas, later killed by the Pokot in 1992.

The next morning found us up early and quickly sipping the *chai* prepared so graciously for us. We left mid-morning to head back to Orus; however we got stuck six times and did not make it back that night. Darkness came as we were digging out for the sixth time and we decided to camp at a deserted Turkana village.

On a later occasion, pilot Jeremy West dropped off the evangelists in unreachable areas of Pokot and Turkana. The teams always took tea and food with them to help their hosts. On this particular trip Evangelist Reuben had brought tea, sugar and cornmeal; a massive *sufuria* (metal cooking pot) of *chai* was prepared. The Turkana hosts told the evangelists they would serve them in the huts assigned to them for the night. After waiting 10 minutes Reuben went back to the campsite only to find their Turkana hosts had drunk the tea, taken the remaining food, and fled into the night!

Our camp that night was located near where Kanyuman was staying with three of his wives. As we talked with them in the evening, we played Gospel tapes in the Turkana language. Kanyuman then waxed eloquent as to what a great host he was. He told how he always killed a goat for his visitors and gave them lots of milk and *ugali* (cornmeal). Jeremy agreed with him, saying, "This is true what you have said because we have seen this great hospitality. But there is still one Person you have not received into your home and life. He is this Jesus whom you have just heard about on the tape recorder."

Kanyuman's response was astounding: "From this day onward I want Jesus to live in my *boma* and go with me on all my safaris." This was his cultural way of receiving Christ.

That evening as we enjoyed the spectacular starlit sky and listened to the hyenas call out, we rejoiced for what we were privileged to experience in the heart of Africa.

Our tents were spread out over a couple hundred feet and placed under the small acacia bushes to get shade in the daytime. Our daughter Kristin was working in Kenya at the time, so she was with us and her tent was the farthest out, but close to the helicopter. We turned in early after a tiring day.

Next morning we looked for lion tracks as we had heard their sounds in the night. To our surprise we found two sets of lion tracks that had circled the helicopter and were less than 100 feet from Kristin's small pup tent. We were excited and thankful for God's protection during the night.

The following year Kanyuman moved to Nasokol, closer to Pokot. We visited him often and shared the words of the Bible with him. During his stay in that area eye doctors from Kapsowar Hospital together with AIM Dr. Ann Fursdon came by helicopter to have a two-day clinic at Kanyuman's village. Over 200 patients were seen, both Pokot and Turkana. Many eyelid surgeries were done, turning the lashes out to prevent scratching of the eyeball. Dr. Fursdon treated many other ailments as well.

Little did we know or understand that our help to the Turkana was not appreciated by the traditional Pokot and we were unaware of a sinister day that lay ahead.

In January 1992 some Turkana from Kanyuman's area (he had moved back to the hills above Napukut) went on a raid near

Kapedo, on the border of Pokot and Turkana. Not only did they steal livestock but they killed an old honorable Pokot diviner.

Pokot warriors with AK-47s in the 1990s.

It didn't take long for the forces of evil and revenge to rise up among the Pokot. In March the counter attack came as the Pokot attacked and stole hundreds of cattle from the Turkana. But worse still, they killed Kanyuman, blaming him for the cattle raid!

Things only got worse after that. There were raids and counter raids taking place.

The Peter Jackson Story

On June 21, 1992, the Turkana raided the Orus area, stealing thousands of cattle. Peter Jackson, 19 years of age and the son of missionary friends Julian and Rachel Jackson, was working with us as a volunteer at Orus.

While attending a dedication of the new Africa Inland Church at Kabartonjo, a place in the Tugen Hills where some of AIM's earliest missionaries were posted in the early 1900s—the Dalziels and the Stewart Brysons served there—we heard the shocking news that Peter Jackson had been killed.

The President of Kenya, the Honorable Daniel arap Moi, was the chief guest and himself a Tugen from that area. He had first heard the Gospel from the Dalziels.

When the service ended, AIM missionary Peter McCallum and I were called to speak with the head of the Kenya Police, Chief Inspector Kilonzo, who informed us a missionary had been shot and killed by the Pokot at Orus. We couldn't believe that. If a raid had taken place there, the Turkana would be the culprits.

We decided Peter McCallum should go to the Catholic Hospital in Eldama Ravine to identify the body that had been taken there by a young Irish priest from Tangulbei, Father Michael. Mary Ellen and I traveled to Orus immediately to get more details. We left for Baringo Lodge where we had left our lifelong friends John and Patty Stauffer with their daughter Ruth while we attended the all day church function.

The Stauffers made trips to Kenya for many years. We had just been on safari with them in northern Kenya. Our original plan had been to stay at Orus for the weekend but the wedding at Kijabe of missionary friends DG Haase and Doreen Wall on Saturday caused us to amend our plans. The Stauffers stayed at Baringo while we spent Saturday night in Nakuru at the Kunste Hotel with Peter and Mary McCallum. Long-term missionaries, they spoke both Kipsigis and Tugen, having served in Sitotwet and Kapropita. They were often called to see the president or to attend functions with him in the Baringo area.

On Monday Mary Ellen and I drove to Orus where the area inspector of police met us. His first words to us were that the Pokot had killed Peter, not the Turkana. Again, we brushed this info aside and went to find Evangelist Reuben to hear his side of the story.

He told us the Turkana came in the early morning hours taking cows from as deep into Pokot as the town of Tangulbei, on the 'main' road some 18 miles from Orus. "Esther and I hid under the bed and I prayed to Jesus telling Him we are ready to come to heaven," Reuben said.

As they lay there, they heard shouting from Peter Jackson's rondavel, 400 meters away. He heard Peter's voice pleading with the Turkana, then several shots and no more talking. Reuben and Esther waited until daylight and by then other Pokot came by in their pursuit of the Turkana raiders.

Reuben and others went to Peter's rondavel and found him dead on the cement floor. Later they heard the story from Paulo, a 14-year-old herd boy staying with Peter in the rondavel. Paulo explained that when the Turkana broke open the door, two of them went straight for Peter. As they began talking with him, Paulo ran out into the night and escaped.

The full story of Peter's life and death is lovingly told by his mother in her book, **Pete's Story** (available through Africa Inland Mission).

We learned that the evening before the raid, Peter had climbed Malam Tiich, the hill behind the Orus mission station (a Pokot phrase meaning the grass is so plentiful that the cows can't finish it).

Peter was well-known for his love of hiking and his love of communing with God. While on the mountain that evening Peter inscribed on a rock the words of James 5:7, 8. "Be patient then brothers, until the Lord's coming. See how the farmer waits for the land to yield its valuable crop and how patient he is for the autumn and spring rains. You, too, be patient and stand firm, because the Lord's coming is near."

Peter's burial took place in his home country of England, but a few weeks later a wonderful memorial service was held in his memory right at the site of his death at Orus. Julian and Rachel, Peter's parents, attended and gave testimony to God in the sorrow of their loss and impressed upon all that they forgave those responsible for his death. Mission and church leaders came. The Catholic priest, Father Michael, was there. The Gospel of Jesus Christ was clearly given by the speakers.

After the service ended I was taking a dozen of the old Pokot leaders back to Tangulbei. One of them made this remark, to which the others all agreed: "Truly Peter loved the Pokot. He had no cows of his own and yet he died because of our cows. His God, Jesus, must be a great God."

Some had hoped Peter would be buried at Orus. Evangelist Paulo Namunyan said that while Peter's body is not here, his blood was here in Pokot as a reminder to all that Peter's blood was given for Jesus' sake for the Pokot people.

Peter's parents started the "Peter Jackson Memorial Fund" that has already helped scores of Pokot and Turkana men to attend Bible college. These pastors are already doing more than 10 times as much as Peter would have been able to do in taking the Word of God to their own people.

Well Drilling

As we planned and prepared to live in the Orus area of East Pokot in 1985, we felt we urgently needed a couple wells for the local people. We were told it would cost $10,000 per well. So in the fall of 1984 when we were on home assignment in the US, we shared this new ministry area with our Evangelical Congregational churches. We explained to a mission conference in Johnstown, Pennsylvania, that we felt inspired by Isaiah 41: 17-20: "God will provide water for the people in the deserts . . ." We gave them the figure of $10,000 per well, also explaining the area was so vast it needed two wells.

Glenn Weaver and Bob McElhattan talked with us after the service and said they could buy a drill rig and ship it to Kenya for less than $20,000. And that is exactly what they did!

Glenn and his wife Wilma came to Kenya later in 1985 along with Lester Henry; they drilled four wells, but initially only found water in one. The following year we went 200 feet deeper in one of their wells and got lots of water.

Glenn, who comes from a family of drillers, told us about his aunt's father who had gone to Mozambique in the early 1900s to build a drill derrick for oil. He drilled 1500 feet, taking a year, but he got no oil. For his return trip to the US he was booked on the ill-fated *Titanic* but his ship into England was a day late and he missed that connection.

In our drilling work we were reminded early on of 'Murphy's law'—if anything can go wrong, it will! Murphy was reportedly a well driller. In our 25 years of overseeing drilling machines in Kenya, we have laughingly found this to be true.

A big factor that is sometimes downplayed by westerners is that spiritual forces often play a part in much of the opposition to missionary work. A place called Kadokoi in East Pokot is one such place. The first time we went there to drill, in 1987, the local diviners put a curse on our efforts. In retrospect, we saw that we did not garner very much prayer support for success in well drilling. Our western minds figured the combination of scientific identification of where to drill, good machinery, and a top notch longtime driller (Yohana Makumbi had been drilling wells for 50 years) would always get water.

Lester Henry, Bob & Autumn McElhattan, Glenn & Wilma Weaver (L to R)

We drilled three holes there, lost one nice 10 inch bit and only got one well with one barrel of water per day. We returned 10 years later with a brand new rotary drill and drilled three more holes. Each hole ended up in an underground cave, empty of water. Again, these were well-identified water sites by the Catholic water department.

Another well was at Katungura, the very first place we drilled in 1985. Glenn and Wilma Weaver and Lester Henry from western Pennsylvania came over with the completely overhauled percussion rig. We went quickly to 265 feet, but then the donors had not sent a long enough bailing line; we left the well and went back to Orus where we got three barrels of water a day and made the decision to build our house there.

The fascinating thing about this well at Katungura was that Earl Andersen, an experienced water geologist, told us we would get some water around 380 feet, but a lot more at 415 feet. A year later a Dutch company came to Pokot to identify where to drill wells for the Kenyan government. They would always ask, "Where did that 'old man' (Andersen) say there was water?" Then they would measure there and confirmed two of the three sites he identified. But interestingly enough, at the Katungura site, they told the Pokot, "There is no water here."

Glenn returned to Kenya in 1986 accompanied again by Wilma and another couple, Bob and Autumn McElhattan. They went first to Katungura and hit water at 385 feet. At 415 feet we struck a large source of water. It was slightly warm, but the best tasting water you ever drank.

Oddly, after we built a generator house, put a pump down and showed the people there was lots of water, the next missionaries who came to the area never followed up on developing this well. In fact, the local people destroyed the pump house. And to this day, there is still a good source of water there, but with no one to develop it. Another factor is that the evangelist posted there did not stay long, instead moving back to Kokwo Toto, a nearby area where there was a church already established.

Glenn and Bob also got a real 'gusher' at Kokwo Toto, where Earl Andersen had identified the place to drill. The estimated flow from this well was and continues to be 13,000 gallons per hour.

Later, in 1994, after the rig had dug dozens of wells all over Kenya, including Mombasa, Turkana area, and Kijabe Mission Station, Glenn's brother-in-law Bob Hurrelbrink came with his wife Emmy to repair the rig and to replace many crucial parts. We then drilled a more permanent well near Orus mission station that continues to provide water.

In 1995 Paul Land of World Mission donated a smaller rotary rig to our program and we soon started to get many more wells, dug more quickly, and at shallower depths. We dug several wells in Pokot, four in Samburu and dozens in western Kenya where water can easily be reached at less than 200 feet.

Another instance that no doubt had more to do with 'money grabbing' than opposition from the traditional religious leaders was at Nyangori in Luo land. The water surveyor from Kakamega told us we would get water at 100 feet and more water at 150 feet. We drilled 230 feet and got NO water. This same surveyor had told us if we didn't get water there, we could instead drill at the high school plot where he had found another site with water. We later learned he was on the board of that school.

We asked the Catholic surveyors from Nakuru to confirm where the water was located. They identified a place only 30 feet from where we had drilled the first well and we got lots of water. But then we lost the hammer down that hole. After that, there may have been an earth tremor and we lost most of the water as we had not had time to put the casing down.

Also connected with this 'Murphy's law' was another driller who came to help to retrieve the hammer, instead deceiving us out of some equipment and over 100,000/—($1300) cash.

And so the work goes on, with great successes and some losses. We have seen our machines drill over 200 wells and help churches, mission stations, hospitals, Bible schools, children's homes, church leaders, community projects and many others to get lots of good water for their needs.

Water is coming out of wells at big stations like Kijabe and small stations like Churo in East Pokot, in highly developed areas like a girls' high school in Kakamega and remote areas like South Horr in northern Kenya.

Twenty years ago we drilled a well for the well-known rancher and author Kuki Gallmann. In exchange, she paid for the drilling of a well at nearby Kaptuya. Francis Chesang, the assistant well driller erroneously identified—and without confirmation from a bona fide geologist—where to drill. The team spent nearly a year, drilling to 600 feet, but never got water.

Several years later we asked Dilly Andersen (son of the renowned water finder, Earl Andersen) to look for another site at Kaptuya. Dilly told us where to drill and several months later we got lots of water at about 550 feet. We went deeper and at about 600 feet struck a literal river of water. When we put our testing bottle down, it hit water at 300 feet. When it reached 600 feet the bottle got pulled forcibly for several meters before we stopped it. Then we pulled against the flow with much effort and finally got the bottle to the well entrance and pulled it up.

We were to install the pump the next day, but upon returning found that some rogues had filled the well with sticks and rocks! It was election year in Kenya and the incumbent Member of Parliament had paid for a generator and pump for this well and the opposition did not want him to tout this achievement. The sitting MP won the election and within the next year we came back and finished the job with much effort and our personal donations (as was often the case).

Now the Pokot are pumping 3,000 liters an hour with a diesel generator and a five-horse-power pump. The well is supplying a primary school, two churches, large gardens and 100 local people living in the community. And for us, the true thrill is that the churches are strong and there is great unity in working together.

We have used Kenyan teams for both rigs for nearly all the wells, but eventually some of the workers saw how they could personally make a profit by not reporting all the wells they dug. We were told they dug five wells, when in fact 10 had been drilled. So we lost a considerable amount of funds that we desperately needed for repairs.

Our long time AIM friend and my RVA colleague Herbert (Dilly) Andersen has done the survey on many wells for us, as his dad Earl Andersen had done. Dilly helped us with wells at Kijabe, in Turkana and Pokot. In 2010 Dilly went to Tanzania to help missionaries there; he identified locations for 36 wells and all of them got lots of water. Dilly gives all the credit to Christ for his giftedness in this area.

At another well in East Pokot at a place called Koisaro, we met the hardest rock ever. It took two full days to go only one foot. And the rock was five feet thick, so it took 10 days total. Finally when we broke through that, we met a huge cave with a lot of wind coming out of the hole. It was like a wind tunnel, but sadly no water.

Wells in Africa often replicate the situation we had at a place called Ntepes in Samburu, just eight kilometers from Ol Poroi. We got good water at 160 feet, but went to 190 feet and put in an India Mark II pump to get maximum water. The pump worked fine. We had agreed with the community and the evangelist Stefano that the people would pay two shillings per 20 liter jerry can, but no one ever paid anything.

The Samburu getting water from a well drilled at Ntepes as a result of the Davis's helicopter safaris in about 1995.

Two years later when the pump rubbers wore out, they had no money to buy new ones (the cost was only 2,000/ for rubbers and the labor to replace them). When I refused to buy them, the pump sat dormant for several months until the next dry season. So then some angry warriors decided they would break the pump, pull out the rods and fill the hole with stones and debris. That took far more effort than it would have taken to replace the rubbers!

They reverted to the age-old way of digging deep holes in the sand for water, sometimes as deep as 20 feet.

By contrast, 30 miles away at Nairimirimo in Samburu, we dug a well 10 years ago and it is still working. It is brackish water, but still drinkable. It is mainly used for the livestock.

Nairobi Robbery

Was this how my 25 years of missionary life was to end in 1997 with a bullet in the head by a bunch of thugs who wanted money? And they weren't even going to kill me for my faith in Christ!

Three days previously we had returned to Kenya from a four-month home assignment in America. At the time we were living in a two-story flat in the heart of Nairobi (or 'Nairobbery' as we jokingly called it). The gunman had ordered me to my knees in our bedroom on the second floor. It was about 8 pm. It was now an hour or so after six thugs had burst into our flat, tearing apart nearly everything we owned. Mary Ellen was being held in a separate bedroom.

Finally in desperation the gunman threatened me, "If you don't tell me where you have hidden the million dollars, I'm going to pull the trigger." This was now the third or fourth time he had asked where the money was hidden. We suspected the reason he used this figure of $1 million was to give me the chance to say something like, "I only have $100, 000," or at least tell him where some money was hidden.

I really thought I was going to Heaven and would see Jesus face to face in the next instant. Again I told him slowly and firmly that we had no other money in the house, only the $600 he had already taken. He said that was not enough and pulled the trigger! The gun went 'click.' I couldn't see his reaction, but felt he became nervous. His voice changed. He quickly told the others to bring Mary Ellen in from the other bedroom.

She came and was forced to kneel beside me. Then he ordered his friends to look again and asked angrily why they were taking so long. We could hear the thugs ripping couch covers and breaking the tile off the side of the bathtub; they had also searched in the small freezer and in the flour and sugar canisters.

Mary Ellen and I began to sing hymns softly to help calm ourselves, realizing this was not going to end quickly. Fortunately, they did not harm us at all at any time. The one in charge, though, did order us to stop singing. Finally, after two hours, the gunman told me to take them away in my car. I had heard many horror stories of people being forced to drive thugs into the forest and then being killed. So I quickly offered my car keys to them instead!

"How do we know you don't have an alarm system on the car?" the gunman asked. I showed him quickly how to disarm the alarm and he sent one of his lieutenants off to start the car, but he stayed behind still holding the gun to my head. After what seemed like a very long time, the others returned saying the car would not start. So I explained that because it was a diesel engine he needed to hold the key on for sometime before turning it all the way on. Soon I heard the car running smoothly and I was overwhelmingly relieved. Someone yelled up the stairs and immediately the leader and a sidekick left.

We stayed in the upstairs bedroom another 10 minutes or so to ensure they really were gone. Then we slowly walked around upstairs, then downstairs to look around there. We quickly locked the door. After a brief prayer of thanks to God for surviving, we decided we should tell our neighbors what happened. There was a small house in the back of our compound occupied by an Ethiopian student at Daystar University and a Rwandese mother with her two young children. They reacted in shocked disbelief, but before long they were praying with us and comforted and encouraged us.

After an incident such as this, mission policy stated we needed to meet with the mission psychiatrist who asked us if we didn't feel angry or revengeful against our attackers. But we had no such feelings, and as Scripture says, we readily forgave our attackers and felt no reason to take revenge.

By the time we left Pokot in 2008, we had seen over 30 churches planted among the Pokot. Over a dozen church buildings had been built and there was a thriving membership of over 2000 baptized believers. We were also blessed to have friends and donors put up dispensaries at Amaya, Churo and Kokwo Toto. They also helped us to start five primary schools. Paul Land from World Mission paid for a Christian high school to be built at Churo in the mid-1990s.

A Muslim imam welcomes World Mission founder Paul Land (right) and his pastor near Lindi in southern Tanzania 1996. Art Davis is standing on the left.

During the first 10 years, we struggled to get just four churches established and only two wooden structure buildings put up, one at Churo and one at Amaya. But after we moved to Orus in 1985, our Evangelical Congregational Church in the US helped us build several more churches with teams from the US coming out and actually doing the building.

The helicopter ministry accelerated the church planting process and the building of churches during a period of over 10 years. As new congregations sprang up from these remote area visits in Pokot and Samburu, the people wanted buildings where they could gather to worship as the dry dusty climate or the heavy rains in the rainy season made it hard to continue meeting under trees. In addition, a visionary Bible teacher, J. L. Williams, raised funds to build three churches in Samburu and four in Pokot.

The church in East Pokot now has 20 trained pastors and over 40 evangelists posted to these churches and outreach preaching points. And as it says in Acts, "numbers were added daily to the church," as these pastors, evangelists and church workers lead more people to Christ.

Chapter 6

Hunting Adventures

During the 1920s and 1930s missionary men hunted to supplement their meager salaries. In those glory days of big game hunting in Africa, the sport was enjoyed by ardent trophy hunters, royalty, wealthy businessmen, big game hunters and movie actors. While they paid huge fees to hunt for a month or two, missionaries, as residents, paid little for their licenses.

Kijabe Mission Station was ideally located on the border of the heavily forested escarpment where elephants, buffalo and giant forest hogs abounded and the sprawling grassy plains of the Great Rift Valley below were covered with plains antelope, gazelle, zebra, lion and jackals.

From Kijabe the men could climb the hills behind them and shoot elephant, buffalo, and giant forest hogs without paying a fee. Or they could walk to the plains below Kijabe and shoot eland, kongoni, gazelle, zebra or warthog for meat for themselves and other missionaries. They often sold the meat to help make ends meet on their meager and erratic missionary income.

My Aunt Florene's Dad, Fred McKenrick, makes missionary life at Kijabe sound like a hunter's dream. Fred would get up at 4:30 am and hike to the valley floor, shoot three kongoni, and be back at Rift Valley Academy by 10 am for a full day's work. His Kenyan trackers and skinners would stay behind, gut out the animals, and carry them home to Kijabe. On another day, Fred hiked up the hills behind Kijabe and shot three giant forest hogs, the biggest one weighing 610 pounds.

Dr. Propst, Mr. Devitt and Mr. Paul Lehrer often trapped lions and leopards on lower Kijabe station. Mr. Propst was so delighted when he finally trapped a leopard that had been eating his pigs!

Grandpa Elwood loved to go out on hunts just to get away from the heavy workload at the hospital, but he did very little actual shooting of animals. He was an observer and recorder of details. On one hunting trip with Dr. Propst to get meat for the station, he records the following story:

"Mr. Propst and I went hunting for meat for the station. They were putting in telegraph poles to Narok. The poles were cedar and they put 19 poles to a mile. Mr. Propst shot two kongoni after considerable walking. We got home at 7:30 pm."

In his most descriptive manner, Grandpa tells of his longest African hunting safari with Harmon Nixon and Roy Shaffer as they went to Maasai to collect zebra skins.

"On Friday, September 16, 1928, we left in two cars, Nixon's and Shaffer's. We signed the police book at Narok at 9:20. We reached the Guaso Ngiro (sic) River (now spelled Uaso Nyiro) at 9:50 at 17.2 miles from Narok. We came to a fork in the road and decided to go left toward Sigana (now called Siana) Springs.

"We had three native workers with us—a Maasai, a Kikuyu and a Kamba. The Maasai would not eat meat, salt or fat. But he was the best worker. Mr. Shaffer had borrowed Mr. Randall's .256 rifle. He got the first animal, a warthog. Mr. Nixon shot a Tommie (Thompson gazelle). Then Shaffer shot a zebra.

"We made a thorn bush *boma* (corral) around the camp as we were setting up. We put up most of it in a heavy rainstorm. Shaffer had also shot a wildebeest and he dragged the carcass off a ways and tied it to two trees to use as lion bait. We took the cars a little ways away for the workers to sleep in. But they were afraid in the open cars and climbed up in the trees to sleep.

"We waited in the thorn tree corral for lions to come. In my 'humble estimation' the main deterrent to lions coming was the loud snoring of my companions. Though I kicked them often it did not stop the music.

"The next morning Mr. Shaffer went and shot a wildebeest. When we went back later to collect it, we found 140 vultures and storks around it (one must remember that Grandpa was a great one for numbers and details, so if he said 140, that was the exact number!). On the way back to the *boma*, Mr. Shaffer shot another wildebeest and we skinned it and put it in the car as well. We found a campsite at Sigana Springs and set up camp. We slept in the front of the car on mattresses with mosquito nets over us.

"The next day, September 18, was Sunday and we had a church service at the *dukas* (small shops). There was an unusually tall Maasai there with scars on his face and head that he had received in a fight with a leopard. A person of such fearlessness and courage in fighting a leopard would be a fine warrior for the Lord Jesus Christ. Would that we had many like him to fight the devil.

"The next day I stayed with the car at Boundary River while the other two went hunting on foot. I heard 22 shots and learned later they had killed eight zebra. This place was 81.6 miles from Siyapei. We found a campsite and had lunch. Then the men went out again and shot seven more zebra (total 15). The skins were later sold for 70/—shillings each—not a very good price.

"I served the supper of soup, guinea fowl and prunes at 7:40 pm. We stretched a canvas over the two cars. The back of one of the seats was used for a table—laid between the two running boards. One of us sat on a cushion on the running board and the other two sat on a box and a *debe* (a 4 gallon square metal tin)."

On another hunting safari on the Maasai Plains in the Great Rift Valley, Grandma Bernice wrote this moving, beautiful letter to her older son Linnell who was far away in America:

"I saw flowers, blue and purple, pink and crimson, scarlet and yellow. There were occasional tiger lilies with their spotted flowers. At times I would see a wax white lily-like flower and others of ivory whiteness. I saw white nodding clusters of little flowers. So even on the dreary (dry season) plains, God has prepared some beautiful sights for those who have their eyes open to see what He has created.

"I am sending you a little pink flower that I picked and pressed. In this little flower, you have a part of Africa. It grew from the soil of the Maasai Reserve. It had the African sunshine upon it to make it beautiful for you to see. It has experienced the cold and darkness of the African night and it has had African dew on it. And now I am sending it on a long journey to give pleasure to my dear big boy in Arkansas."

Grandpa Davis regularly treated wounded hunters for injuries received during their hunts. On one occasion he treated an English 'landed gentry' for a broken collar bone, suffered when he was attacked by a rhino. Another time a professional hunter came whose arm had been chewed by a lion. The lion was killed by the client, and after a long recovery time the professional hunter went back to hunting.

On September 27, 1928, he writes, "We treated a man mauled by a leopard which he and a friend had wounded. He and fellow hunters thought it was dead and so went after a second one. When they returned for the 'dead' one, it jumped them. It was mauling this patient's arm so he put his hand down the leopard's throat; the second hunter came and shot it."

On Friday, November 9, 1929, Grandpa writes of another hunt. "We started looking for eland (on the plains below Kijabe). As we searched the plains below us with glasses (binoculars) I saw a herd of eland looking at us. Propst shot at a bull and hit it and it dropped behind the others. We finally caught up with it and shot it again. When Propst went to get the car, he heard from the natives that another herd of eland had gone by. And then Propst saw them and there was an even bigger bull in that second group. But he didn't shoot it, as he couldn't take two eland (at 1,500 pounds each) and the people and loads in the car."

Interestingly, some 45 years later on the plains beyond Tangulbei in East Pokot, I was on a hunt with Dave Huber, my father-in-law. We shot two eland and using our 109 Land Rover station wagon, we were able to carry both back to Amaya where we were building a mission station.

During my earlier days at RVA in the late 1940s it was almost a monthly event for Mr. Lehrer, the homemaker, to trap and shoot a leopard or lion. It was a big day for us kids to see these magnificent and dangerous beasts. Because of the danger these animals posed to the increasing native population, the government asked Paul to kill them and turn the hides over to government officials.

Several times Mr. Lawson Propst and Welles Devitt walked up the hills above Kijabe to shoot elephant. I was still a student there in the 1950s when Welles Devitt and Lawson Propst's son, Dr. Jim Propst, shot an elephant. The whole student body of 100 kids hiked up to see this majestic and mammoth beast with Propst and Devitt perched on top, guns in hand. Hunting meat for the school at Rift Valley Academy and for other missionaries and conferences, as well as some to sell in order to buy other necessities, had been a part of life in the 1920s and 1930s and most of the men loved the hunting. But by the 1950s and especially after the Mau Mau native uprising, hunting for 'survival' became a thing of the past. Instead, it became hunting for fun and for trophies. By the time I was old enough to hunt in the late 1950s we enjoyed hunting and looked forward to hunting trips for months.

The biggest animal I shot (when I returned as a missionary) was an elephant. But the whole ordeal was fraught with delays, disappointments and I almost lost the income from the tusks. In the 1960s several missionary men went out nearly every vacation and shot one or two elephants. The income from the ivory could pay return airfare for their families to the States.

Also in those days, the men were getting large-tusked trophies, with some weighing 100 or more pounds per tusk. Many were taken with 70 and 80 pounds per tusk.

When I came along with an elephant license in 1976, we only managed to get one with 50 pounds per tusk, but the pair was beautifully matched and very symmetric with only one pound difference between the two tusks. Howard Berry and I bought one license between us as the cost was so high we could barely afford

From Foot Safaris to Helicopters

it. We borrowed some money assuming we would get an elephant quickly and be able to repay the loan immediately. It took more than a year before we got our elephant and paid back our loan!

Having bought the license, we went off for a week with a qualified elephant hunter back-up (as required by law), John Pelletier, a missionary kid from Congo, who was a world-class artist and a very careful and safe hunter.

We traveled to the delightful Doldol Hills of Samburu just northwest of Mt. Kenya and set up camp. After we shot an antelope for supper, we sat around the fire listening to stories of past elephant hunts from John. We knew we were with the right guide.

Next morning we were up before dawn and out on an elephant trail. John had carefully instructed us not to shoot at an elephant until he gave the word. We came close to several good trophies—probably 60 or 70 pounds in each tusk, but John would not let us shoot them.

We found out later he was trying for a bigger elephant than he had ever shot and didn't want to take anything else. His strong passion to supersede any of his previous records came back to haunt him and us, because a week later hunting was banned for a year (and it could have been a permanent ban)!

When elephant hunting was finally re-opened a year later for a limited time to enable license holders to fulfill their quotas, we went on a couple hunts.

One was with famed missionary hunter Winston Hurlburt (grandson of Charles Hurlburt, first AIM General Director in Africa), who had shot bigger tuskers than any other missionary and most professionals. He had hunted in Congo, Uganda, Sudan, Kenya and Tanzania and had bagged several with tusks of 120 or more pounds each. Win has one of the biggest sets of tusks that he ever bagged in his home in Arizona. But many other tusks he had sold to pay for his visionary missionary tasks.

We traveled to the border of Tsavo East in Win's old short wheel base Land Rover. It was like old Africa. His stories held us spellbound. His bush craft was unsurpassed. He insisted we all take target shots with his huge .458 Winchester magnum. But after Paul

Jorden, son of Dr. Paul Jorden, took a shot, Howard and I decided since Paul was to be the hunter, there was no need for us to try. We decided this after observing the way this large gun nearly sat this tall and muscular man on his haunches when it fired!

The next day Win picked up the tracks of a lone, huge bull and his immediate comment was, "This bull has over 100 pounds in each tusk." He explained how the size of the footprints and the space between its steps showed it to be an old bull with very large tusks. We were filled with excitement, hope and determination. But as we followed the tracks, Win deduced this big boy had already gone far.

"He is probably over 100 miles from here by now," he said, as he showed us the way the imprints were made indicated he had been moving at a good pace.

To our dismay, Win decided not to follow the elephant to try to catch up to it. We never saw another elephant that day or the next and had to head home without firing a shot.

Finally, toward the end of our available time to get an elephant, we booked two hunting blocks with another well-known hunter and artist, now a famed sculptor, Dave Schaefer. Dave had many big tuskers to his name, but he too wanted one last 'Big' one to add to his stories. We booked block 41 along the Samburu and Rendille border at Ilaut and the bordering block 40 near Ngurinet.

We hunted all day in my block without seeing any of the mighty pachyderms. So we moved to Dave's block in the later afternoon. At nearly dusk, we finally saw a small herd of silent forms moving across the semi-desert. The wind was in our favor and the *tembos* were moving right toward us. We were on top of a small rock hill *kopje*, so had a great view. When they got to within 500 yards of us, they took an abrupt ninety degree turn and headed toward the hills and dense bush. Dave was not happy with this, but said that our only chance, and it was a risky one, was to come up behind them on foot. So we climbed down off the rocks and moving as quickly and quietly as we could, we approached the herd of about 15, some with good-looking tusks. When we were less than 100 yards behind them, Dave instructed me to shoot at the lead elephant on the right, which seemed to have the biggest tusks. I fired from a standing position. Dave and another friend, Dave Entwistle, fired also. We all reloaded and fired a second time. The herd disappeared into the dense acacia tree forest on the run.

Dave said we could not follow them in there in the fading light, but he was sure we got the big bull and we would come out the next morning and find it. Sure enough, at the crack of dawn we came back and found the big boy 'down and out.' Already a lion had eaten away some of the meat from the head and stomach and must have just run off as we approached. We quickly removed the tusks, the four feet, the ears and the tail and left by 10 am. We spent the night on a ranch near Nanyuki, then reached Nairobi the next day, mission accomplished.

But it was to be nearly another year before the government released the tusks for sale and we finally got our money to pay what we had borrowed for the license fees and our costs for the hunting.

Colin Jackson, the brother to Peter who had been killed at Orus, told us of his non-hunting encounter with elephants. He and two friends camped high in the majestic Aberdare Mountain Range at about 10,000 feet. He and the others had cooked their supper over the campfire, and then retired to their thin nylon tent and warm thick sleeping bags for the night. Around 2 am they watched a huge lone bull elephant circle their tent not once, but twice, plucking at the guy ropes as it went around, as if to taunt them before starting to pull the tent apart. He then picked it up in his trunk with the three lads inside, swinging it around and dropping it and them 15 yards away! Colin felt a huge weight on his right shoulder and realized the elephant had its foot on him. When his collar bone and shoulder blade cracked, he passed out and came to outside the tent (there was a 'Jackson-shaped hole' in the screen window). Looking up he saw the elephant's head silhouetted against the stunningly moonlit night sky—he was directly under the elephant's head and still in front of his feet. The elephant was just bringing his tusks down to explore the tent further and Colin briefly held on to one as it passed him. "In my stupor I guess I just wanted to say 'thanks for treading on me, *rafiki* (friend)!' to the elephant," Colin remembers. As his predicament came into better focus, Colin leapt up and away from the elephant and ran behind the car shouting and screaming. The elephant wheeled around, thankfully not over the other two who were still in the crumpled tent, and then ran off into the night.

It seems it was the scent of the delicious plums inside the tent that brought the elephant. Fortunately for Colin, he only received a broken collar bone and cracked shoulder blade. One friend was knocked unconscious and the other suffered just a bruise—he was the one who drove Colin the two-and-a-half hour drive to Kijabe Hospital from the campsite.

Hunting stories from Africa have filled many books. I am just highlighting some of the hunts of our four generations of missionaries and their colleagues. For example, our dear friend, missionary and honorary game warden George Machamer had numerous thrills as he hunted and killed all of the Big Five. He took me hunting several times when I was an older teenager. On one trip we hunted the elusive and beautiful lesser kudu. A large buck weighs 230 pounds and stands four feet six inches at the shoulder. He has a dark gray coat with white stripes and a tawny mane. We were in an area George knew well and where the kudu could be found. As we walked stealthily through the waist high golden grass, peering intently on all sides, we were suddenly confronted by four lionesses less than 100 yards away.

In all my hunting adventures, my heart never beat so hard and so loud! George and I had two guns and the tracker had none. We could easily and quickly have been dispatched by these four hungry-looking beasts (perhaps descendants of the legendary man-eaters of Tsavo). They started toward us, looking like they would love to have us for supper!

"Don't move," George whispered. "Stand your ground and take aim at one of them." No sooner had we lifted our guns than they bolted through the grass and out of sight.

But a couple weeks later George was not so fortunate on a rhino hunt. And I was glad not to have been with him. George had successfully put away several of these unpredictable beasts in past years and was following all the rules of bushcraft as he stalked this quiet partly-hidden beast about 70 yards away. The wind was in George's favor. He was well hidden by other bushes and rhino are reputed to not see very well anyway.

But without warning as if he had been waiting for that precise moment, the brute burst forth from his hideout and came right at George. George didn't even have time to aim his massive .458 weapon, but shot from the hip, hitting the rhino somewhere in the middle of its body.

Seconds later the rhino's horn clipped George's gun right out of his grip and sent it flying; the impact also sent George sprawling. The rhino 'turned on a dime' and came at George, who was now lying on his back. George kicked him in the snout repeatedly. The two-ton beast's most sensitive area is his nose. So after several blows the wounded rhino, perhaps also bleeding internally, seemed to lose interest in burying George into the sod and ran off.

George was severely bruised and couldn't walk well. He and his tracker slowly made their way back to the car a half-mile away. He just managed to get into his pickup and painfully drive the 15 miles home; it took days to recover fully.

Over the next couple of days his trackers followed up on the wounded rhino and found him dead. They brought the horns back for George. But George's reaction was, "From now on, I'm going to be a birdwatcher." And a very successful and renowned birder and bird photographer George became, right up to the time of his death in September 1988.

But the most significant part of George's life was the spiritual impact he and his wife Dorothy made on a segment of the Kamba population from Emali to Mtito Andei and from Makindu, their home, to Ikutha; and even in later years at the coast where they lived for some time and then in their latter years in Nairobi.

Today there are scores of churches scattered throughout this area, with thousands of believers and hundreds of pastors and evangelists, thanks to the Machamers' more than 40 years of missionary work in Kenya, most of it around Makindu.

Echoing the theme of this book, *"if it's really true,"* the Machamers and their many believers in Christ undoubtedly are another example of the certainty of that truth which has sent bearers of the Good News of Jesus Christ around the world, not only in this past century, but ever since the resurrection of Jesus Christ.

When I hunted in the late 1950s in the area around Makindu, I had a dozen close calls with charging rhino. But after one got used to their manner of charging, it became less dangerous.

The very first time I was charged, I was with Paul and John Barnett, twin brothers who also became missionaries like their parents. We were looking for antelope such as oryx, impala, kudu, bushbuck and kongoni as well as the tasty warthog.

We were walking along a dry riverbank, hoping to scare out a bushbuck, kudu or warthog. Erik Barnett, Paul and John's father, and the tracker were walking down the riverbed and we were waiting downriver to nail anything that burst out of the bushes. To our great surprise there was a big rustle in the bushes just below us and out came a fully grown rhino, snorting and mad! We couldn't shoot it because we didn't have a license for it. But we almost had to shoot, just to protect ourselves.

The brute came right up the riverbank to where we were walking. John and I climbed a small thorn tree, getting jabbed many times. There was no time for Paul to climb, so he faced the rhino with his .375, ready to shoot. The rhino reached the top of the bank, saw Paul right there in front of him less than 10 feet away, and quickly turned around, running back down the bank and then the riverbed. Paul did not have to shoot. But, boy, he was shaking like a leaf!

In a nearby area a year later when we were hunting antelope with Henry Hildebrandt we got charged again by a rhino. In those days there were so many rhino that we were charged at least once a day and sometimes twice. Henry and I had spotted some zebra on the next hill and were making our way towards them. The tracker was in front and pointing out animal tracks, when suddenly he stood up, turned, and bolted past me all in one blurred motion.

We instantly saw why—a rhino was coming right at us! Normally it would have been 'curtains' for both Henry and myself, but because of having been charged several previous times, we quickly darted behind a bush just as the rhino went by. Due to a rhino's unique eyesight perception, he doesn't know in which direction you flee so as long as you drop out of sight you are okay.

People who hear such stories usually think we are exaggerating or stretching the distance and time elements. But those who hunted in rhino-infested areas in those days know how the 'cat and mouse' rhino dodging was carried out on every hunt. Since rhinos are so big, so uniquely created, so unpredictable and especially so rare these days, I can never tell enough stories about them and how I came to really enjoy seeing them in the bush, especially as they charged away after missing me!

Several times when we hid behind a bush that wasn't even big enough to stop a dog, yet were out of sight, we were also out of the rhino's mind; and hiding behind a bush became our way to avoid being attacked by these unusual beasts.

John Machamer and I were stealthily walking through the green grass and dense bush when right behind me I heard the short and heavy hoof beats of a huge rhino. I saw him out of the corner of my eye and bolted forward—only to trip on a root and fall flat on my face. To my utter amazement the rhino went off to the left; the reason again being that I had disappeared from his sight and he saw no enemy.

I had some good hunts in Tanzania with several hunters. One was with Bill Snodgrass and Simon Long. In his farmhouse in Pennsylvania, Simon has two large rooms displaying his game trophies from around the world, including full body mounts of the African cape buffalo, lion and rhino, polar bears, musk ox from Mongolia, Alaskan brown bear and other antelope and cats.

Simon was just a 'plain old dairy farmer' but he really loved hunting and spent every spare penny and a lot of his time during his latter years to fulfill his dream of hunting everything everywhere. Even towards the end of his career, it was exciting for others to see him so thrilled to bag a kongoni at 350 yards. His wife Reta was so supportive, encouraging to Simon, and patient during his many safaris away from home.

Perhaps the most enjoyable and relaxing hunting I had in Tanzania was with my brother-in-law Bob Leaman, who is one of those rare human beings who is content with simply shooting a couple guinea fowl out of the air. At the same time he is so casual about bagging the world's most dangerous game animal, the African Cape buffalo. With professional guide John Mongi, Bob managed to do both on this delightful and fulfilling hunt on the high steppes of the Maasai plains in Tanzania.

Bob and I camped simply in tents with John's cook providing our meals. We ate our meals under a tree, surrounded by the expansive African thorn tree savannah full of game animals and as evening approached we enjoyed the beauty of God's creation as the beautiful red-hued sunsets showed through the silhouetted thorn trees. At night we heard hyenas and jackals which set the dogs to barking.

Especially after about the second day when Bob had gotten several trophies and there was lots of meat in the camp, the predators were never far away. And our only annoyance during our week-long stay was the incessant barking of the dogs at night!

One morning we enjoyed an ostrich egg omelet for breakfast. The one egg was enough to feed six people. We ate lots of game meat—always the best cuts of fillet. And, of course, we drank lots of tea. John also served fruits such as papaya, pineapple and mango. We ate well!

But the best part was being out on the hunt. Bob was not one to want bigger, better or more out of a hunt. He was content with one or two good trophies. He was so easy to please and pleasant to be around.

One of the highlights of our hunt was when an orphaned baby zebra ran up to our car, hoping it was its mother, and followed us for a long time. It came right up to the car several times. Finally John had his tracker chase it far away. We feared for his life alone on these predator-infested plains.

Bob shot a very large impala buck with long wide horns. The pictures tell the story of the trophy. But it was Bob's good marksmanship that made it so easy. He almost always downed his trophy with one clean well-placed shot. There was no need to track a wounded animal, nor did we have a limping suffering animal to follow for miles.

Bob was able to get a couple impala, a nice-sized Grant's gazelle, a duiker, warthog, oryx and a cape buffalo. We shot the good-sized bull buffalo at 6 pm—not a preferred time to bag this brute, especially if you only wound him and have to go after him in the fading light. But it was the last day of the hunt and I so badly wanted to see Bob get one of the most coveted trophies that we agreed to go for it.

Bob and I each got two shots into it and we were sure it would go down. But it didn't, and it ran off with the other big bull into the dense bush. We followed the prints and blood spoor for some time before darkness set in. Our guide John Mongi suggested we return in the morning to get it. We returned to camp a bit disconsolate. But John assured us we would easily find it the next morning and still be able to take the trophy out with us.

We set off at the crack of dawn to get Bob's trophy. When we reached the area where he had gone into the bush we were a bit fearful as we had heard so many stories of a wounded buffalo waiting to finish off his adversary.

Slowly we followed the blood drops and tracks with our guns loaded and the safety off. It always amazed me to see how far a buffalo can travel with a huge .375 or .458 bullet in his body. But if the bullet does not hit a vital spot he can live for days and even years, and do great harm to the next unsuspecting hunter. Because of that concern we wanted to find the buffalo. We also really wanted to get the trophy and take some photos. After spending a couple of hours tracking our quarry, the bush became more impenetrable and the danger multiplied with every step.

Finally John decided we must give up the hunt for our own safety's sake. We readily agreed. John told us he would have a couple Maasai who lived in the area notify him when they found the dead animal.

Sure enough, by the time we got back to Nairobi, John called to say they had found the dead buffalo not far from where we had stopped tracking it. "And it is a pretty good trophy," John added. "It's got a 40 inch spread on the outside of the horns." It was to be over two years before Bob finally got the trophy in Pennsylvania and had it mounted. It now hangs on the wall of their family room.

Great Hunting Experiences with a Great Friend

Undoubtedly some of the most memorable and bizarre hunting experiences are ones I shared with our good friends John and Patty Stauffer.

We met Stauffers in 1967 before they married later that year. John was going for a PhD in Communications at Syracuse University and Patty was studying for her master's degree in education. In 1968 John and I had the good fortune to be part of a literacy seminar in Nairobi, Kenya, and Patty traveled with him.

John and Patty fell in love with Africa and when Mary Ellen and I came back to Kenya in 1972 as fulltime missionaries, John and Patty visited us nearly every year. They loved Kenya so much they took leaves of absence from their teaching jobs in the Boston area to work for two years in Kenya. John taught journalism at the University of Nairobi while Patty taught in the primary school at Rosslyn Academy, also in Nairobi.

We did a lot of safaris together. On one hunting trip at the foot of Mt. Kilimanjaro in Block 23, we were interested in some zebra and other plains game trophies. We had rented a camper Land Rover. One morning we began to see some really unusual zebra. They had far more black than white in their stripes. We drove closer but never were able to get the zebra to stop long enough for me to get out and shoot.

Finally after a couple miles we came around a bend and out of the trees; there in front of us was Ol Tukai Lodge, the first and most famous of the Amboseli Game Park lodges. We had seen no sign showing the park boundary, or any indication that we had left our hunting block. Normally, there is a rusty half of a 44-gallon barrel with the block number printed in white on all the roads as you enter or exit a hunting block.

We quickly hid the guns under the back seat and went into the lodge for lunch and to fill the vehicle with petrol. As we left later we made sure we were quite far down the road before getting out the guns (we were carrying a .300 Winchester magnum, a 12 gauge shotgun and a .22 rifle).

John & Patty Stauffer with Ruth by the Ewaso Nyiro River.

Further down the road we spotted a really good trophy Grant's gazelle. As I was turning the car around and negotiating a big ditch, I broke the rear axle (a common weakness of the old Series II Land Rover). We could only travel in front wheel drive and for some reason only in low range gear. We crawled along at about 20 miles per hour, all the way to the dusty little town of Loitokitok, hoping to find a garage there.

There was a simple petrol station with a couple pumps and an even simpler garage with not much in it. But the mechanic told us his relative had an axle in his *manyatta* (Maasai village of several mud and dung covered huts).

We drove a few miles out of town, meeting his relative who confirmed that, yes, he still had the axle, but only the right (or longer) one. It was the exact part we had broken. In an hour we were on our way again, having parted with a bit of cash for the axle and labor. We had a great few days of camping and hunting, returning to Nairobi with yet another 'unbelievable' set of stories.

A couple years later, this time while John was teaching in Nairobi, he and I went on another safari to Amboseli Park just to enjoy the wildlife and take photos. John was an accomplished photojournalist and we traveled in his short-wheel-base Land Rover. We stayed at our favorite Ol Tukai Lodge enjoying the good food, warm swimming pool and great accommodations, while looking at the massive Mt. Kilimanjaro every day. It was during the dry season, so the view of the mountain was fantastic and the game viewing at its best.

While getting some great close-up photos of two black-maned lions, we did not realize that our right rear tire had gone flat until we tried to leave. We then had to stealthily get out of the vehicle on the side of the car away from the lions and as noiselessly and quickly as possible jack up the car and change the tire. God is always looking after His 'brazen' children and we managed the job undisturbed by the lions.

The next day we got bored with photographing so many elephant, buffalo, and prides of lion and rhino that we decided to go off on our own into a remote part of the park to find some new adventure. We came on a set of lion tracks. We decided to follow the tracks until we found the lion. So off we went, sometimes moving quickly and at other times getting out of the car to look hard for the tracks. But we always found the tracks until one particular place where there was a fairly large grassy bushy section maybe 200 yards across. So unwittingly and unwisely (stupidly!) we said, "Let's each walk around a different side and find where the tracks come out."

When John and I met on the far side of the bush he asked, "Did you find where the tracks came out?"

"No," I replied, "did you?" John also replied in the negative. So, rather frightened, we concluded the lion was still inside that bush and we better walk back together. We got our Swiss army knives out as our weapons and rather quickly returned to the Land Rover.

From Foot Safaris to Helicopters

We had to confirm the lion was in there so we drove the Land Rover into the grass. Less than 30 yards in, sure enough, a fully grown lioness bounded out of the grass in front of us, disappearing over the plains. God's angels surely protected us that day!

Once the Stauffers wanted to hunt for the rare and beautiful grevy zebra. So we arranged a safari to one of the northernmost hunting blocks in Kenya, number 65, which included the very hot area of the Kaisut Desert.

As we traveled in our old Land Rover station wagon in the heat of the day, the car suddenly stopped on one of those northern dusty roads. There was no other vehicle around and it was just John, his wife Patty and I. John and I got out, opened the bonnet of the car, and started fiddling with all the wire connections. Nothing seemed out of place.

I remembered the trick my parents had learned on safari in 1959 when a Good Samaritan had used tin foil from his cigarette box to tighten a connection in the distributor. (You can read that story in chapter 7). Mary Ellen had packed some tin foil for us and I crumpled up some and put it in the right place in the distributor and it solved the problem! The car engine started right up and off we went. We did hundreds of miles in this northern desert and the old 1961 Land Rover took us all the way.

On one hunt we bagged a lone grevy zebra at the end of a long day and after a very long and tiring tracking experience. Whenever we'd come close, the large old stallion sauntered away. Sometimes we needed to go on foot to pick up the tracks. Other times we dodged gullies and bushes to keep on its tail.

At about 6 pm as the shadows from the scrawny thorn trees started to get much longer than the tree, we had to go for a really long shot. I got a good position behind a thorn tree, resting the barrel of the gun in the tree, took my time and slowly squeezed the trigger. The zebra was facing directly away from us and as the bullet exited, it took off like a horse out of a starting gate, running hard and dodging among the bushes. We thought I had missed completely. We went back to the car, jumped in and took off in the direction the zebra had run.

When we reached the spot where the zebra had been standing, we saw no evidence of a hit, no blood on the ground. We got out and started tracking on foot. After 100 or so yards small blotches of blood began to appear on the ground. We got back in the car and started following the tracks. Because of the fading light we wanted to go at speed. After about half a mile, to our immense surprise and joy, we found the magnificent stallion lying quite still.

A fully grown stallion weighs 800 pounds and so it was a huge job to load this heavy animal into the back of the Land Rover. It was dark when we took off and the next challenge was to find our way back to camp on this roadless desert. We finally made it, very weary, but very happy. We were too tired to skin the large animal that night, especially as it takes great precision to remove the face mask without spoiling it.

The beautiful skin of this animal today adorns the floor of the Stauffers' living room in Bonita Springs, Florida, and is a nostalgic reminder of the good old days of hunting alone in the great wild north of Kenya before the arrival of bandits and elephant and rhino poachers.

Perhaps my hardest and hottest hunt was in the desert of Baragoi with my 75-year-old father-in-law, David M. Huber. We set off from our home in Amaya and headed north to a hunting block that was little used, due to its barren landscape and distance. We were particularly looking for the northern beisa oryx, a 650-pound lithe antelope with up to five-foot-long scimitar-like horns.

As we approached the desert area we saw a nice herd of over 50 oryx, so we thought our safari would be over quickly. But when we tried to approach the herd off road on the open weed-tufted terrain, they took off. On several attempts we couldn't get closer than a half mile from them. We decided to go over the hill and set up camp out of sight of the oryx.

There is nothing like the late afternoon and evening on an African desert. The temperatures drop; the features of the hills, the sparse thorn acacias, and even the boulders, take on a subdued hue of changing colors and character.

We enjoyed eating roasted partridges and *ugali* (corn meal) and sipping our tea, all prepared over an open fire, and then watching the cloudless brilliant starlit sky of the African night. Our plan was to get up early, have a cup of tea, and before daylight sneak up to the area where the oryx had been.

The predawn came all too soon, but our cook-cum-tracker, Joseph Mengich, had a pot of steaming hot tea for us when we got out of our tent. We sipped it slowly and felt its warmth and sweetness energize our bodies.

As we took off towards the oryx, the dipping moon provided just enough light to see our way. We walked over a mile, keeping well below the ridge where we had last seen the oryx. As daylight quickly dawned over the cooled-off desert, we slowly climbed, looking constantly for the oryx.

Suddenly there they were, grazing contentedly, facing away from us. The wind was in our favor, but we were still half a mile away. My father-in-law was a great hunter, a resilient wiry man who would attempt anything. So I told him we would have to crawl on our stomachs for several hundred yards to get closer and to keep from being detected. Fortunately it was not yet hot as the sun had not come up, and the bushy tufts were easy to worm our way over. But it was not fast going.

After half an hour of snaking over the ground, I dared to ease myself up and take a peek. To my amazement and our good luck the oryx had grazed towards us and were not less than 100 yards away.

I asked Joseph to kneel just in front of Dave to provide a shoulder rest for the gun, and I told Dave he would have to take a quick shot before the oryx spooked. Joseph put his fingers in his ears and when Dave had the crosshairs on the oryx he squeezed off on the trigger.

The oryx dropped instantly and the herd took off in a dusty gallop. We stood up, half expecting the downed oryx to get up and run. But it never did. Dave had hit it square in the middle of the neck. It was a record class trophy with horns over four feet long.

As we traveled back to Amaya through Maralal we reported our trophies to the game department who then asked us to take care of a troublesome lion that had been killing Samburu cows. We went to the area called Losuk, set up camp and set out the oryx as bait. We were really tired and Dave had been coming down with a cold, so we slept soundly. No lion came anyway. But the next day Dave decided he couldn't stay out another night in that cold windy plain so we went home to Amaya, only 20 miles away.

    I could tell more hunting stories, but these are enough for this book.

Chapter 7

Key Partners

We could do little and not survive long without the prayers and support of those faithful, unsung and often unheralded heroes on the home front.

Our four generations of missionaries in Africa and three generations in South America can testify to our 'successes' only because others gave sacrificially and prayed effectually at home on our behalf.

When I was a senior in high school at Rift Valley Academy in Kenya my folks took us to Amboseli Game Park together with Dr. Frank C. Torrey, the pastor of their home church in Lancaster, Pennsylvania, and Walter Himmelreich, a church elder, one of their kind supporters and a close friend.

We had a super time in Amboseli in 1960 on this visit when there was still a lot of game in the park and the surrounding Maasai population was not as large as it is today. The road from Machakos, where my parents lived, to Amboseli was all dirt in those days.

My folks had a Chevrolet pickup and we boys loved being in the back, while our folks and Walter talked about church matters up in the front of the car. Dr. Torrey rode with the John Schellenbergs who were also from Calvary Church. They had a pickup with a specially made back for camping and for doing literature distribution while on safari.

On our way out of the park my Dad's pickup 'died' on the road. Try as he could, Dad could not get it started. We boys thought, "This is great . . . to be stuck in the wilds with the lions and other wild game." But looking back, I now realize it was not so great for Walter and Dad who planned to be with the others back home that night and already had another schedule planned for the next day. In those days there were not any tour vans and very few tourists, so no one came by. Dad said we should eat some snacks we had with us and prepare to spend the night. The African nights are beautiful with rich red sunsets on the hills, but even more so here with the fading sun casting changing colors on Kilimanjaro. The temperature dropped to a pleasant coolness and as dusk crept over the plains the hyenas and jackals started their nightly howls and prowls. We heard the jackals yelping that night and lions roared from somewhere towards the hills.

We huddled together trying to sleep but were more awake and excited with the night sounds. Dad was up early and told us we could all get out to use the 'out of doors' bathroom facilities.

Fortunately for us another early morning traveler came along the road and as everyone did in those days, he stopped to see how they could help. The driver was an English Kenyan (or 'Kenyan Brit' as they are now known). He immediately detected the problem, which was a bad connection in the distributor. He pulled out his pack of cigarettes, opened them and removed the aluminum lining. This he then wadded up, inserting it into the top of the distributor to make a firm connection. The engine started instantly and off everyone went.

Not many people have ever heard of Elizabeth Wetherbe. She has not been featured in mission magazines. She has not been paraded in dynamic missions-minded churches. She is not listed on any mission lists. But all her life Elizabeth has supported missionaries and helped them fulfill their vision through her powerful prayer life and faithful sacrificial giving. There are other mission supporters with big names who have contributed millions to missions. They are widely-known and often praised in mission literature. God uses them all, but it will be very intriguing to see God's records when they're revealed in eternity. The unsung 'widows and their two mites' (Mark 12: 41-44) are truly the backbone of the missionary enterprise. And their prayers are the atomic power behind much of what goes on in the darkest and most remote corners of humanity.

Dr. Paul Jorden is a retired orthopedic surgeon from Wheaton, Illinois. He brought his wife and nine children to Kenya, built a large house to accommodate the family, and contributed a year of his life to the medical program at Kijabe Hospital, while his wife, Janet, taught at Rift Valley Academy. He and his family started a foundation that has blessed many missionaries and mission projects down through the years. Dr. Jorden has authored a very descriptive book, **Surgeon on Safari**, which tells some of the experiences that he and his family enjoyed during their year on the mission field.

Dr. Jorden helped us to purchase our first 4X4 vehicle to use in reaching the remote Pokot and he made several trips there himself with various family members. Besides his medical help, 'Doc' was a great encourager to us and to the young Pokot church. Paul's daughter, Sue, and her husband, Dr. Ben Zivney, picked up on our vision for Pokot; through their support and visits, we were able to reach even more remote areas and start new churches. We hired Pokot men to open up roads far into the bush so we could reach the more remote peoples living there.

As momentum gathered, Dr. J. L. Williams, a pastor, Bible teacher and fundraiser from Burlington, North Carolina, raised funds to build six good-sized churches among the Pokot and three in Samburu; he also gave timely teaching to the leaders of the rapidly growing churches in East Pokot and Samburu.

Our friends the Stauffers have been mentioned in other chapters. Our relationship with them is probably the longest lasting of any of our friends; they are also one of the most generous supporters to us personally and as a family. With their help we were able to do greater things for the Pokot. They also made an annual donation to our kids' college funds and they treated us royally whenever we were together—here in Kenya, in Massachusetts, or later, in Florida. We sure felt spoiled while dining at the Ritz Carlton or on a Caribbean Cruise, or in some of Kenya's 5 star game lodges.

Pat Brandon, a young woman from one of our supporting churches, began contributing towards evangelists' salaries; twenty years later some are still proclaiming the Word of God, thanks to Pat's generosity.

In the very beginning of our ministry in Pokot, while we were still living at Kijabe, Sue Clegg, a young Canadian high school graduate, came to visit a family at Kijabe who was involved in medical work. As part of that visit, Dr. Morley Phillips brought Sue on a medical safari to Pokot. When Sue returned to Canada, she began sending us $10 per month; she continued that practice all through college and into her first job. When she later married Mike Winslow, he also shared her vision, and as a couple they have continued their monthly support towards our work. Later, the Winslows' church, Emmanuel Baptist of Mt. Vernon, Washington, sent teams of young people to participate in ministry among the Pokot; Sue came on one team and another time the entire family came to visit Kenya. As more reports went back to the home church, members of the congregation also decided to contribute towards our work in Kenya.

My folks never had much of a salary. But they did have some faithful givers who blessed them with special 'extras' in their lives. I have told the story of the visit to Amboseli Game Park with the Himmelreichs and Frank Torrey, the pastor of their church in Lancaster.

A couple years later the Himmelreichs treated our family to a tour of the Holy Land on our way to the US for furlough. I vividly remember being awed by the scene at Golgotha, and the empty tomb from where Christ had risen from the dead **"because it is really true"** and we were seeing the same place nearly 2,000 years after Christ's resurrection.

That trip was so memorable that I took our family there twice in the 1980s as we traveled to the United States for our furloughs. Perhaps the most dramatic scene was sitting on the hillside above

Galilee and reading Jesus' Sermon on the Mount to our family. Kind friends assisted in those trips as well.

In the early days, the retirement plans of missions and churches did not provide an adequate amount for their missionaries to live comfortably. Because of that, one family from my parents' supporting church sent them an extra monthly amount. The big boon during their retirement years was that a godly benefactor of the Van Eddings (my grandparents) offered free housing in his spacious and lovely house near Lake Davis in Orlando, Florida, saying they could stay for as long as my grandmother, Gara Eddings lived. She lived for 16 additional years (passing away at the age of 100), enjoying this delightful home with my parents; we missionary families were grateful, too, for this roomy house when we came to visit during our furloughs.

Mr. Williams, who had been an attorney for McCrory's Department Stores in the US, was a quiet, detailed, generous and godly man whom God had blessed. He supported my grandparents generously while they were missionaries in Venezuela.

These and other unsung heroes have kept the Gospel message spreading through the decades, through missionary pastors, doctors, radio programs, builders, teachers, and general missionaries. In all these cases, they were more than supporters; they were often great friends as well.

Churches, too, are really the mainstay of the mission movement overseas. They not only provide sound teaching to their members, they give generously to keep the missionary and his mission board solvent. Some churches are able to give hundreds of thousands of dollars annually to missions. Others can barely keep afloat financially themselves, but they faithfully forward their missions funds to mission agencies. Churches are also the prayer powerhouses for those missionaries whom they support financially. The Evangelical Congregational Churches, with offices in Myerstown, Pennsylvania, have been the mainstay of support during our missionary years.

Calvary Church in Lancaster, Pennsylvania, which supported my parents fully for 40 years, had a policy that half their annual budget should go to missions. Even when they had a major building project, they still maintained their mission giving, sometimes increasing it. When this church began in the 1930s there were just a few families who were members. They took on the full support of my parents and did that at first for everyone who went as missionaries from there. But as the church grew, support costs increased, and more missionaries were being sent out, so they gave only partial support. Two of my brothers and their families (Van and Kathy, Ray and Jill) have been blessed by support from Calvary Church.

Towards the end of our fulltime ministry in Pokot, a couple with whom we had enjoyed only a brief contact in Kenya during the 1970s came back into our lives. Joe and Lori Warren were in Kenya in 1974-1975; Joe taught at Kenyatta University and Lori at Rosslyn Academy. They had been given our names by a church member in Detroit. We got together, having some great safaris together, camping and hunting. On a trip to Churo in Pokot, Joe, a top notch artist, painted the 70 year-old father of Pastor Julius Kiprop. This old Pokot was so colorful and always decorated to the full!

We lost touch with Joe and Lori for some twenty years and amazingly reconnected in the 1990s. From among their friends, they put together a medical team and came to work with us in Pokot and Samburu. This was the beginning of another whole chain of short-term missionaries and donors who have helped us, including monthly support from their home church in Ocala, Florida.

One of the team members, Dr. Sharon Ayabe, has come three additional times for ministry and invited us to her church mission conference in Hawaii. Sharon not only volunteered herself to come to Kenya, but volunteered others to come as well. Dr. Bob Wotring came a few times; Sharon's father, Dr. Harold Ayabe, came and astounded the Pokot with his simple but powerful teaching skills. "We understand everything he tells us," Evangelist Francis Kudokoi remarked. Sharon's sister Cheryl and her husband Randal have also come to help.

On a recent very tough trip, Sharon brought an 85 year-old pig farmer, Uncle Mamo, who probably worked harder than anyone. Dr.

Sharon has the gift of enthusing others for the work they come to do, whether it is treating a patient or building elephant-proof fences!

Every missionary should have a Stauffer family, an Ayabe family, or a Jorden, Winslow, Warren or Zivney family as backers and prayer supporters. They and others have been great supporters of our ministry in Kenya, some since our arrival in 1972.

Conclusion

Probably the best kept secret about Christian ministry—especially missionary work—is that it is mostly a whole lot of fun!

- Tumbling down the lower Amaya River in East Pokot, northern Kenya, on large Land Rover tubes watching animals in the surrounding dense bush; being surprised by guinea hens erupting from the grass in surprise as humans appear; snakes disappearing in the muddy water.
- Going 50 mph across the Maasai plains while chasing warthogs, then almost tipping over and nearly throwing good friend John Stauffer off the roof rack when we hit a warthog hole.
- Sleeping under the canopy of a dark African night lit up by a star-studded sky.
- Admiring the ingenuity and control of the Great Creator as galaxies move silently across the vast expanse of the heavens.
- Appreciating God's protective care when two lions come within 30 feet of us as we are sleeping on top of our flattened tents in the sand.
- Snorkeling along the reef of the clear waters of the Indian Ocean—an unsurpassed marvel! Scenes of color and sea life constantly changing in front of the mask. A sand-colored crab displaying computer-like chips with different colors alternating on top of his shell.
- Myriads of identical copper-colored fish darting in and out of a sea cave, all moving in perfect unison as if directed by the baton of a maestro.

- ❖ A cheetah appearing out of nowhere on the vast undulating Maasai plains. Within seconds he is running at 70 miles per hour, closing in on a darting and desperate Thompson's gazelle; the gazelle escapes; the cheetah stops in a cloud of dust, panting heavily.
- ❖ Observing a herd of majestic elephant moving silently and quickly across a stretch of open plain between two clumps of riverine acacia trees in the cool dusk of northern Kenya mountains. The sun is low behind the Ndoto Mountains, casting long shadows from trees and mountains alike. We are amazed at the purposefulness of the herd of 25 *tembo*.

These are just a few of the thrills and experiences of life as a missionary in Africa. But the ultimate thrill is in knowing that after 40 years of each generation, there are dozens of new churches, thousands of new believers, and hundreds of well-trained pastors and church leaders on the job!

I have been overwhelmed in reading the letters and diaries of my grandparents, Dr. Elwood and Bernice Davis, written during their almost 40 years in Kenya, from 1911-1950.

Truly they did a lot more with many more obstacles and with a lot less than succeeding generations of their missionary offspring. They are role models *par excellence* to those of us who come behind.

They lived on little financial support and experienced privations that are unknown to us today. In a letter to her two sons in America, Bernice decried the fact that they could not send them any money for Christmas. Then she added that perhaps they could send a gift to the mission for an even poorer family that they knew of.

I would have loved to have written volumes about Elwood and Bernice because of their great love for the Africans, their fellow missionaries, and their work. But as the writer to the Hebrews wrote concerning heroes of the faith, "the half has not been told."

We in the generations following, humbly and gratefully dedicate this book to the life, ministry and honor of our beloved grandparents, Dr. Elwood and Bernice Davis.

We have been blessed and privileged to have had you show us the way of a Christ-like sacrifice and dedication of your lives for the sake of others in great need of spiritual and physical help.

For you to live was Christ and to die—leaving such a wonderful legacy—was eternal gain.

Thank you.
Art Davis, for all of us

BIBLIOGRAPHY

Africa Inland Mission. *Inland Africa.* January/February 1917; March/April 1940; November 1926; July/September 1938; November/December 1938

Davis Family Letters and Diaries

Devitt, Edith. **On the Edge of the Rift**, printed in Canada by University Printers Ltd.,1992

Hamilton, Genesta. **In the Wake of DaGama**, Skeffington & Son Ltd., London, 1951

Herne, Brian. **White Hunters,** Henry Holt and Company, New York, 1999

Jackson, Rachel. **Pete's Story,** Eagle Publishing Ltd, UK, 2009. ISBN 086347 381 4

Jorden, Dr. Paul with James R. Adair. **Surgeon on Safari,** Hawthorn Books, 1976

Laubach, Frank C. **Living Words,** Zondervan Publishing House, 1967

Phillips, Kenneth. Retold by Malcolm B. Collins. **Tom Collins of Kenya—Son of Valour,** Evangel Publishing House, 2003

Shaffer, Ruth T. **Road to Kilimanjaro**, Four Corners Press, Grand Rapids, 1985

Glossary of African Words

Words are in Kiswahili unless otherwise noted
banda, n. small house
boma, n. corral, homestead
chai, n. sweet milky tea
debe, n. rectangular metal four-gallon container
donga, n. elongated ditch
duka, n. small local shop
jembe, n. hoe
kali, adj. strong
kikapu, n. woven basket
kubwa, adj. large
lopoi, n. Pokot, everything, all
mandazi, n. triangular donut
manyatta, n. animal enclosure, homestead
Mau Mau, n. an uprising against the colonial government
mlango, n. doorway, opening
morani, n. Maasai, young man
mzungu, n. white person
ngoroko, n. cattle raider
panga, n. machete
rafiki, n. friend
safari, n. a journey
samosa, n. triangular pastry often filled with spicy meat

shauri, n. a matter to be discussed, a problem
simi, n. two-edged sword
sufuria, n. metal cooking pot
tembo, n. elephant
ugali, n. cooked corn meal

The Davis Family Tree

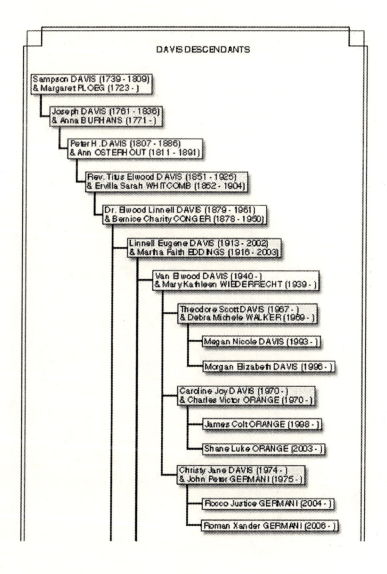

Art Davis

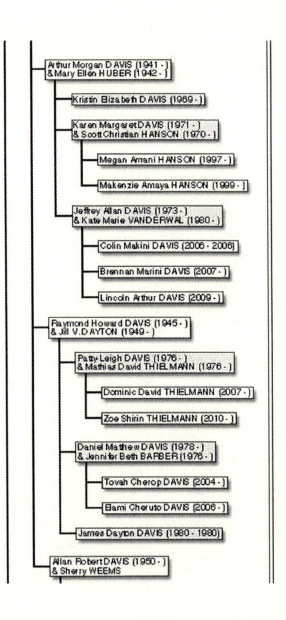

From Foot Safaris to Helicopters

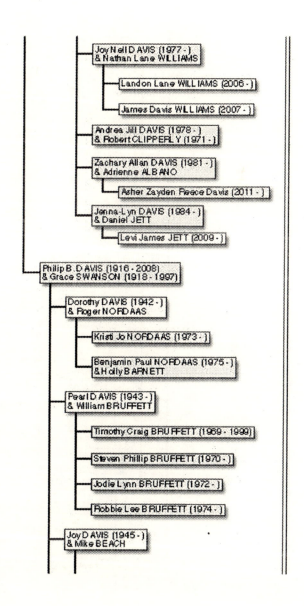

Art Davis

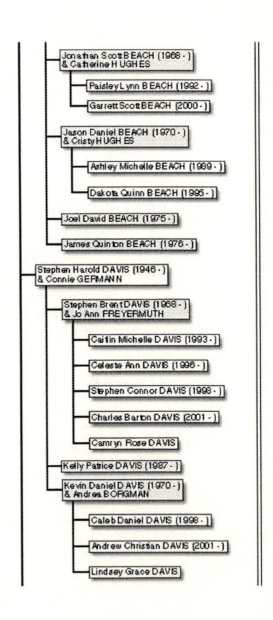

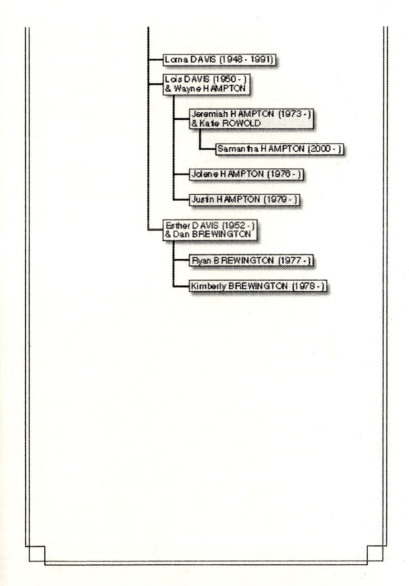

Special thanks to Dave Mills for compiling this information.